Fashion DESIGN SKETCHBOOK

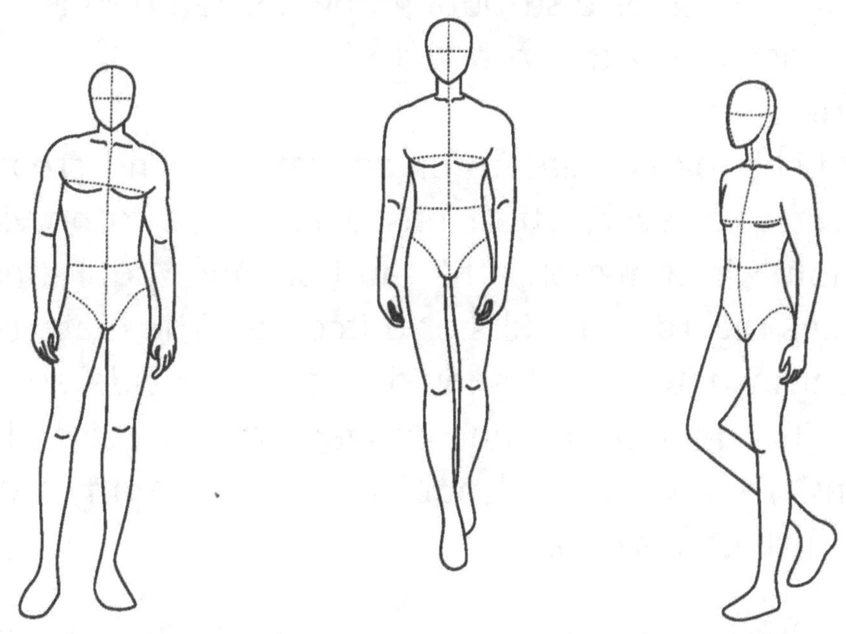

MALE FIGURE TEMPLATES

From Beginner to Advanced

Niky Jadesson

© Copyright 2025 – Niky Jadesson
All rights reserved.

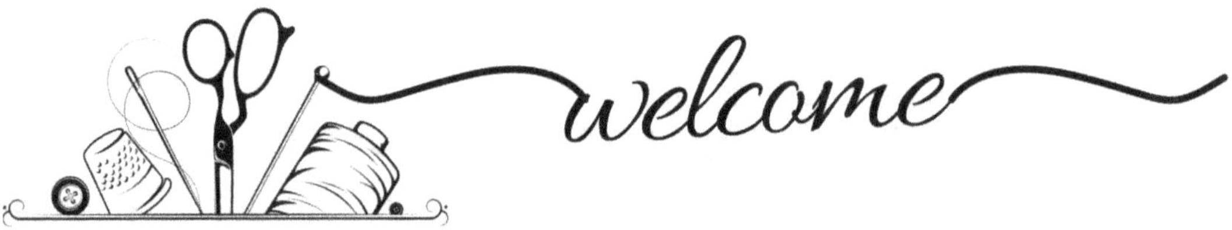

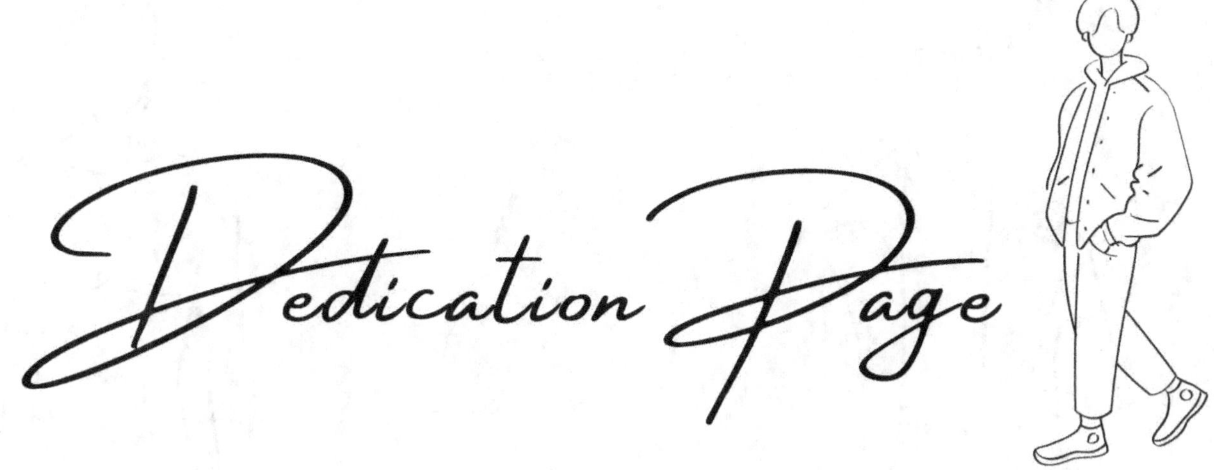

Dedication Page

To every aspiring fashion designer inspired by men's style, tailoring, and creativity.

This book was created for you - to experiment, to learn, and to express your ideas through clothing design.

May each page give you confidence, inspire originality, and remind you that every sketch is the beginning of a masterpiece.

And to the mentors, colleagues, and loved ones who support this journey: thank you for being the true foundation behind the art.

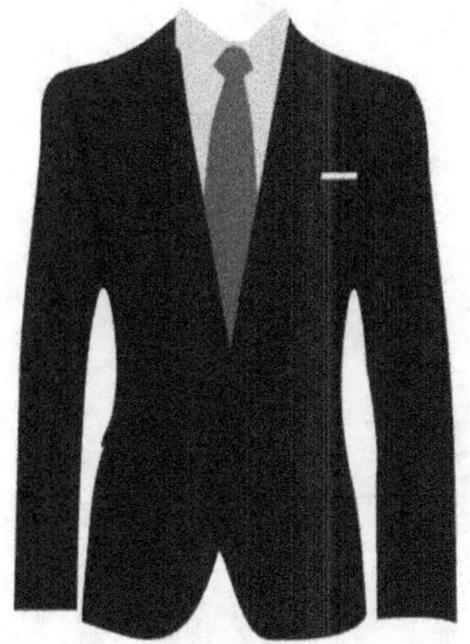

With respect and passion,

Niky Jadesson

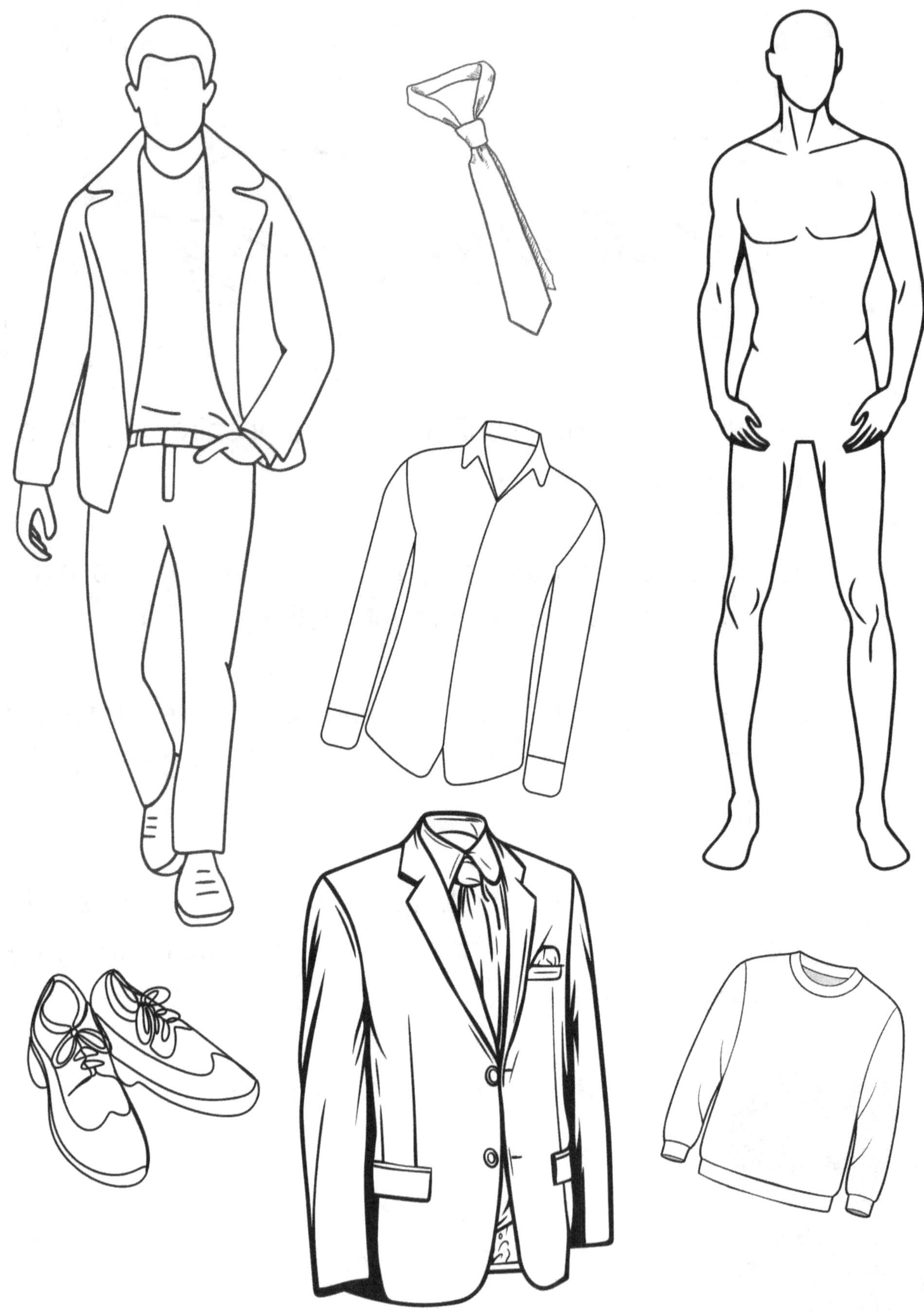

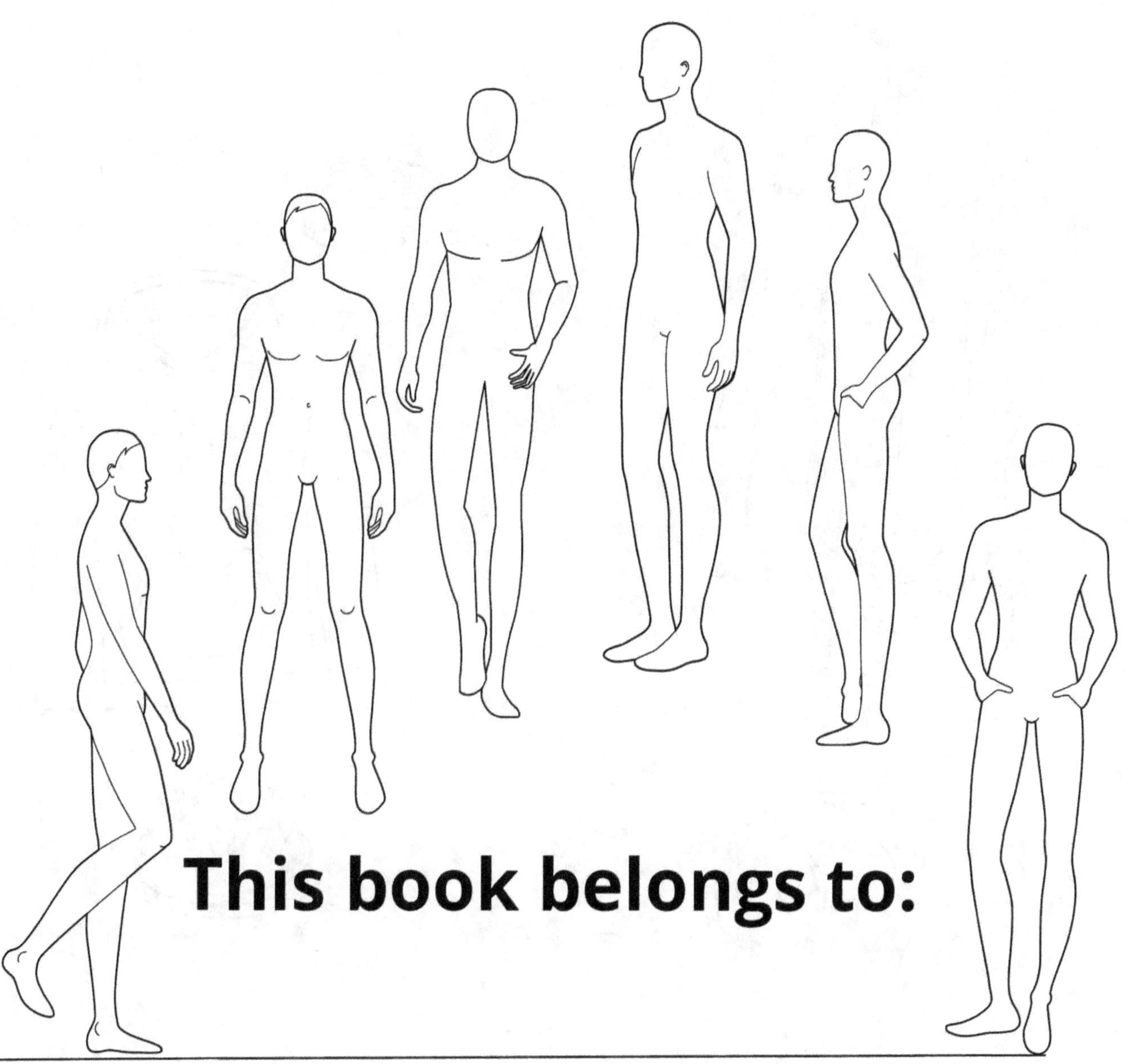

This book belongs to:

____

____
(your name)

Niky Jadesson

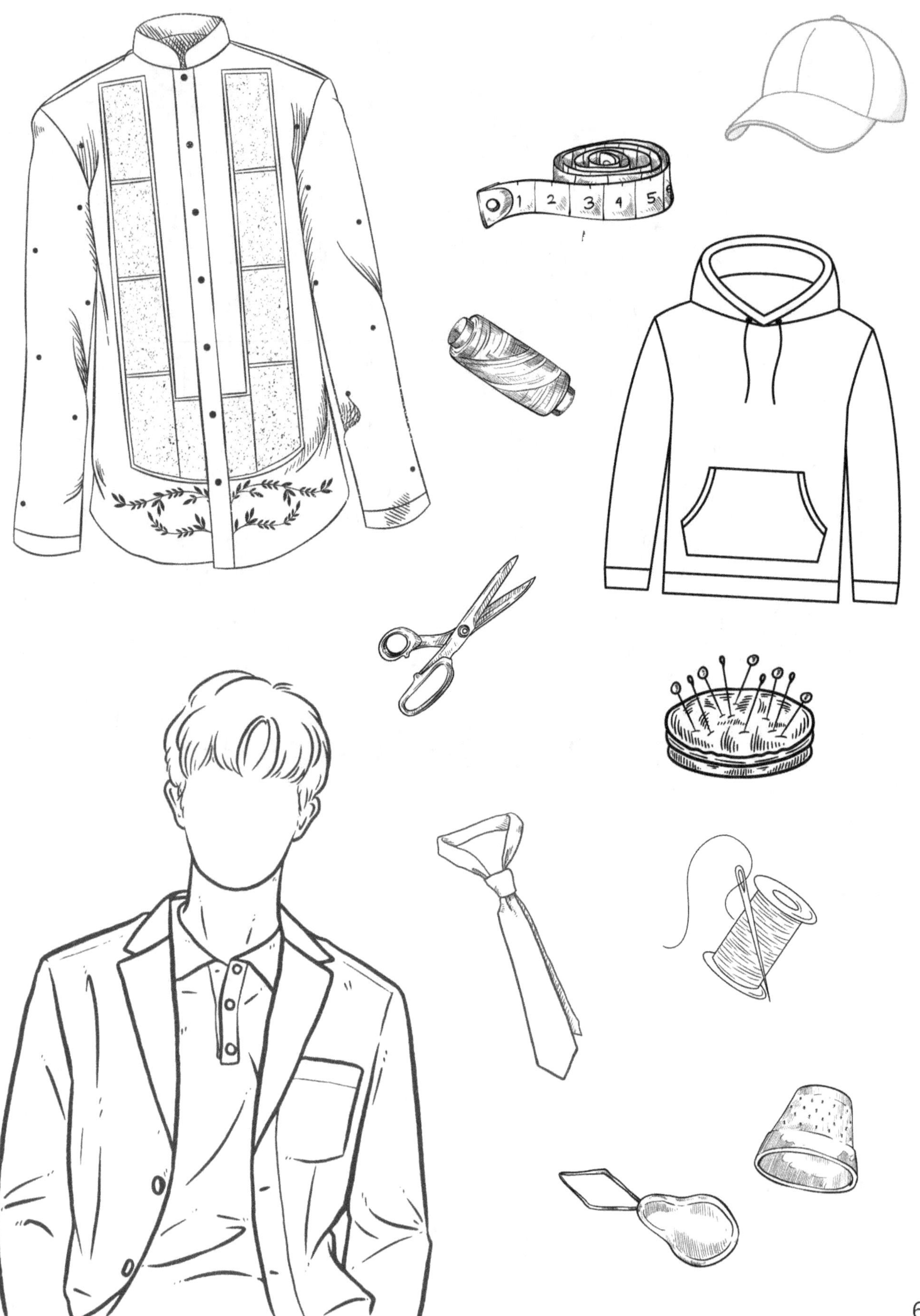

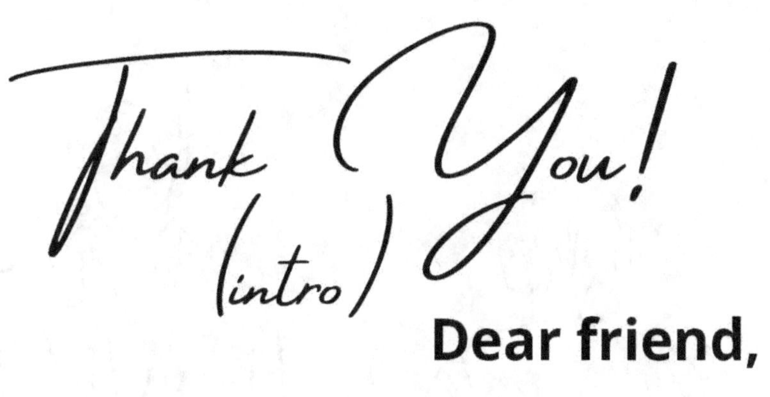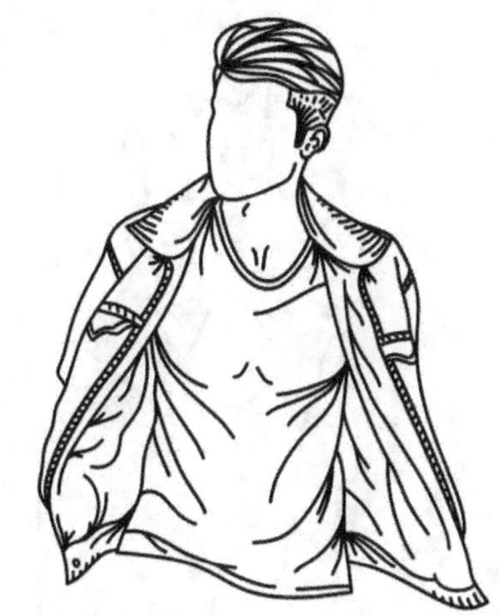

Thank You! (intro)

Dear friend,

Thank you for choosing this sketchbook!

Fashion is more than clothes - it is a language of identity, culture, and creativity. Like every designer, you need practice, inspiration, and the right tools to shape your vision.

This book was created as a space to explore men's fashion, experiment with designs, and grow your skills step by step.

If you'd like to stay updated on future books or share your feedback, you can find **"Niky Jadesson Books"** online.

Your support means the world. If this sketchbook inspires you, leaving a short review helps others discover it and supports independent publishing.

With gratitude,

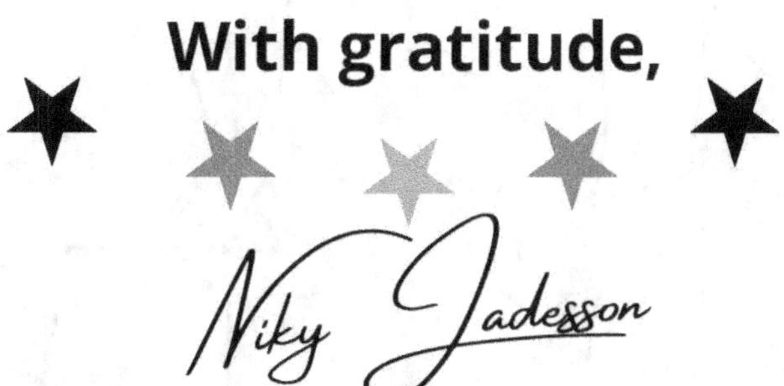

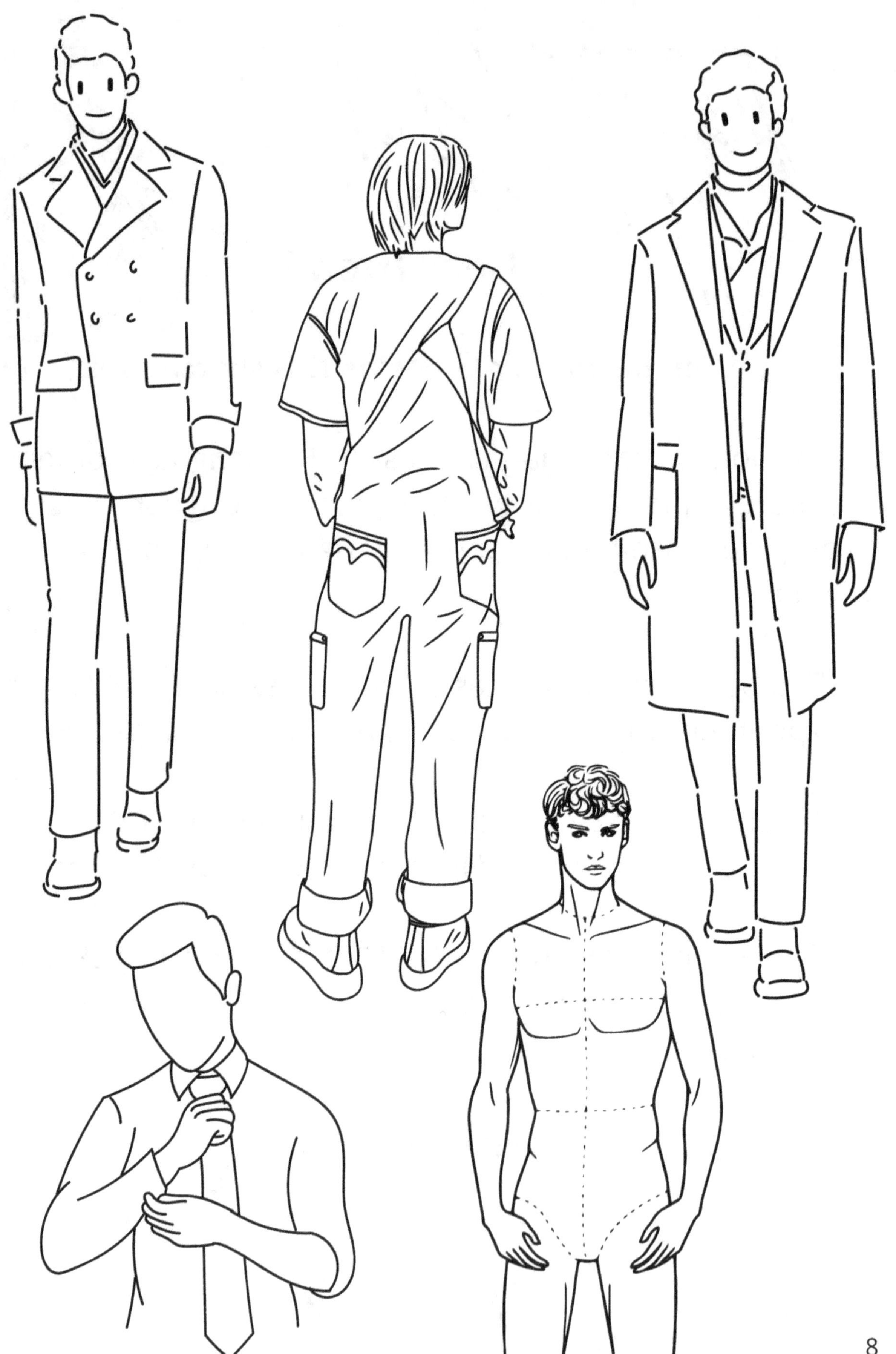

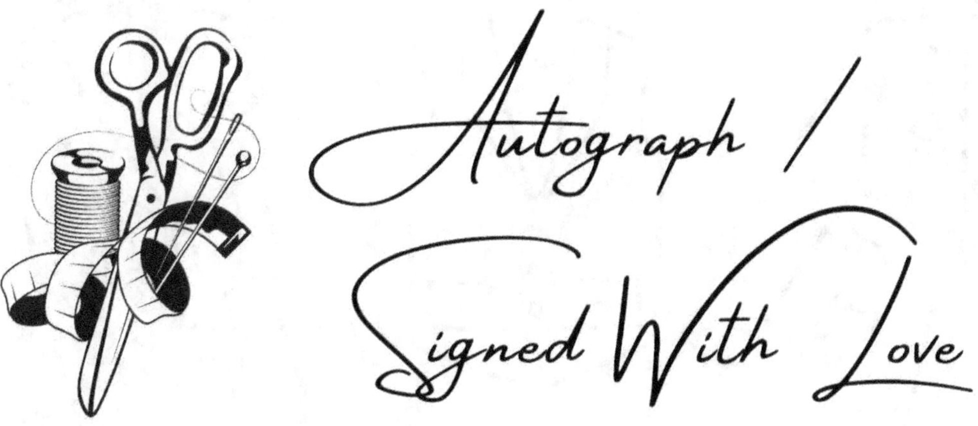

Dear ___________________________,

This sketchbook is for you - to practice, create, and celebrate your vision of men's fashion.

May it remind you that every outfit you design is a step toward mastering your art.

With all my respect,

____

(Signature)

Date: _______________

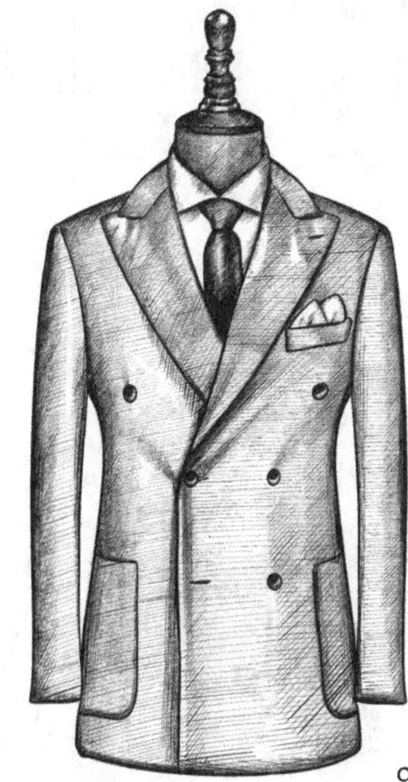

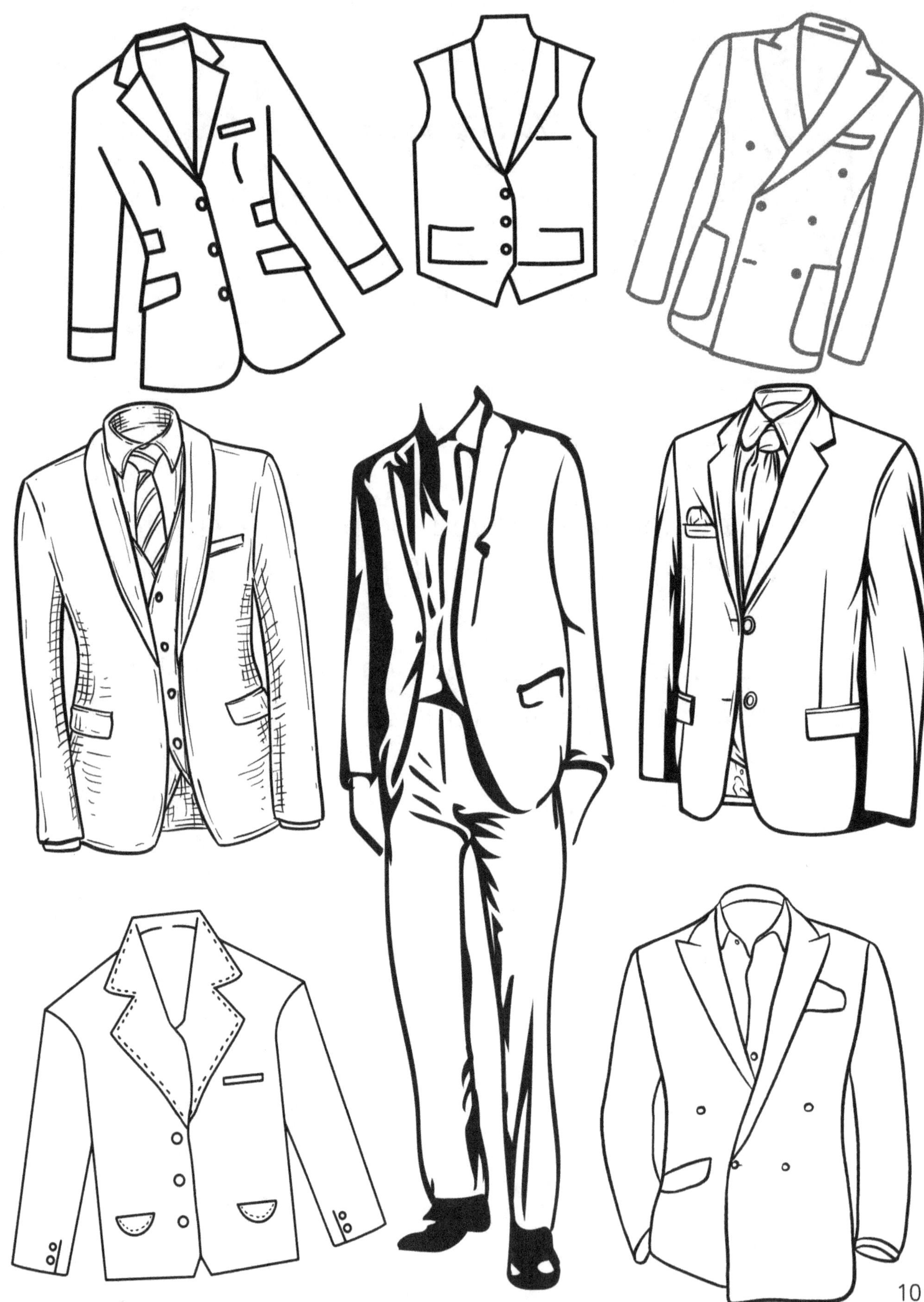

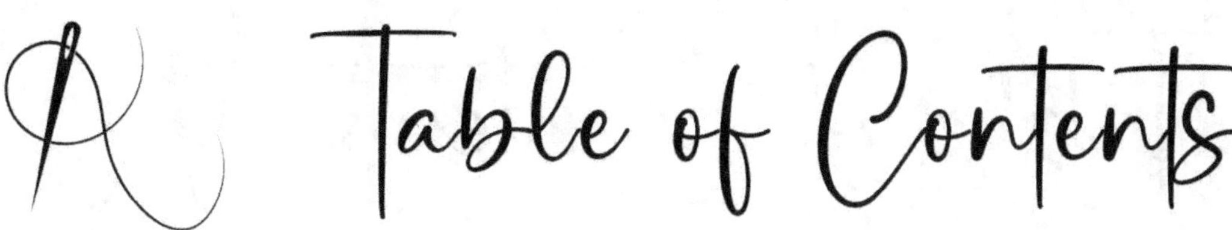

Table of Contents

Part I – Intro Pages

1. Title Page 1

2. Copyright Page 2

3. Dedication Page 3

4. Coloring Pages (Bonus Creative Inserts)..4, 6, 8, 10, 14, 16, 34, 144, 146

5. This book belongs to 5

6. Thank You! (Intro Message) 7

7. Autograph / Signed With Love 9

8. Table of Contents 11-12

9. Welcome! 13

10. Author's Preface 15

11. How to Use This Sketchbook 17

12. My Goals & Inspirations 18

13. Tools & Materials for Fashion Sketching 19

14. Tips for Getting Started 20

Part II – Education & Fundamentals 21

15. A Short History of Men's Fashion – From Classic Tailoring to Modern Styles 22

16. Male Silhouettes Through Time – Slim Fit, Oversized, Boxy, Athleisure 23

17. Color Theory in Men's Fashion – Neutrals, Earthy Tones & Bold Accents 24

18. Fabrics & Textures for Men's Clothing – Wool, Linen, Leather, Technical Fabrics 25

19. Fashion Sketching Tools – Pencils, Markers, Digital Options 26

20. Step-by-Step: Casual Day Outfit (Streetwear or Smart Casual) 27

21. Step-by-Step: Evening Look (Business Suits & Formalwear) 28

22. Common Design Mistakes in Men's Fashion (and How to Avoid Them) 29

23. Tips & Tricks from Menswear Designers 30

24. Step-by-Step Guide to This Sketchbook 31

25. Fashion Sketching Fundamentals: Step by Step 32

26. Quick & Easy Everyday Fashion Look 33

Table of Contents

Part III – Sketchbook & Practice 35

27. Fashion Practice Guide & Notes 36, 44, 51, 58, 65, 72, 80, 87, 94, 101, 108, 116

28. Outfit Inspiration: Streetwear 37, 45, 52, 59, 66, 73, 81, 88, 95, 102, 109, 117

29. Body Templates – Male Silhouettes (Front, Back, Side Views) 38–41, 46-48, 53-55, 60-62, 67-69, 74-77, 82-84, 89-91, 96-98, 103-105, 110-113, 118-120, 123-130

30. Your Notes & Inspiration Photos 42, 49, 56, 63, 70, 78, 85, 92, 99, 106, 114, 121

31. Outfit Inspiration: Business Casual and Runway Menswear 43, 50, 57, 64, 71, 79, 86, 93, 100, 107, 115, 122

★ *Note: The Body Templates – Male Silhouettes and practice pages are intentionally repeated across several sets to encourage structured practice, creative flow, and design diversity.*

Part IV – Closing & Extras 131

32. Body Templates – Male Silhouettes (Front, Back, Side Views) 132

33. Creative Exercises 133-140

34. Fashion Designer Checklist 141

35. My Favorite Fabrics & Brands – Space for Notes 142

36. My Personal Fashion Journal 143

37. Congratulations! You Did It! 145

38. Thank You! (final message) 147

39. Thank You for Choosing This Book! 148

40. About the Author 149

41. Glossary of Fashion Terms 150-151

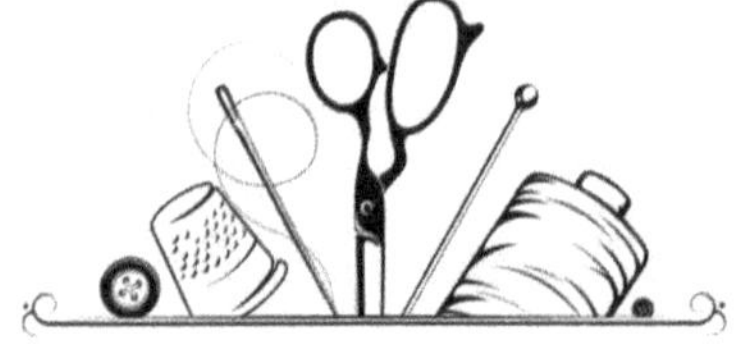

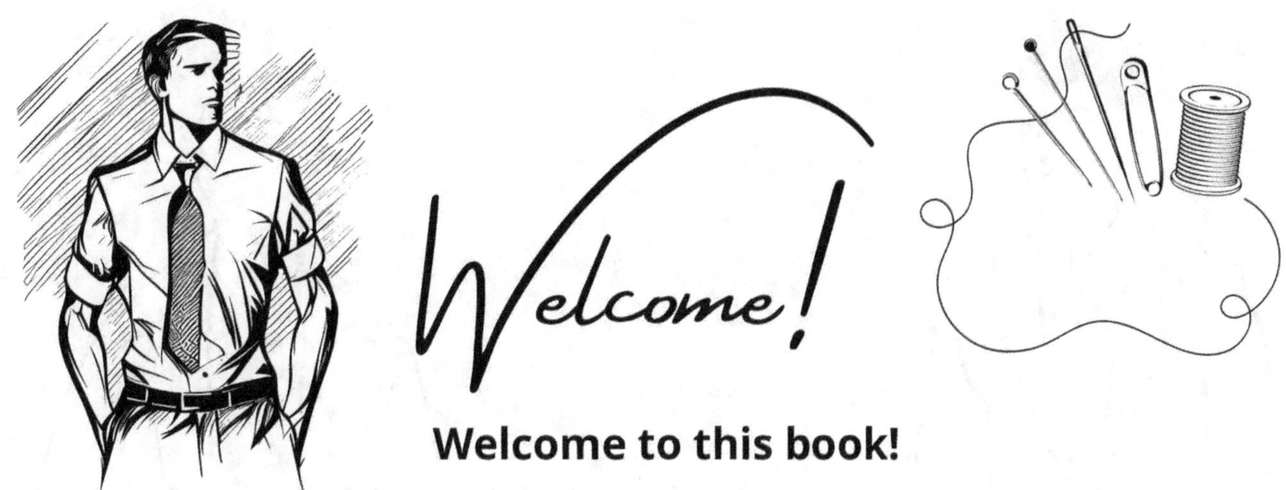

Welcome!

Welcome to this book!

Men's fashion is a world of structure, detail, and innovation.

From tailored suits to streetwear, every design tells a story.

This sketchbook was designed to help you practice, explore, and refine your creativity in men's clothing design.

Take your time, test different silhouettes, fabrics, and colors, and most importantly, enjoy the process.

Whether you're just beginning or already experienced, this is your space to experiment and grow as a designer.

We're honored to accompany you on this journey.

Happy designing!

Niky Jadesson

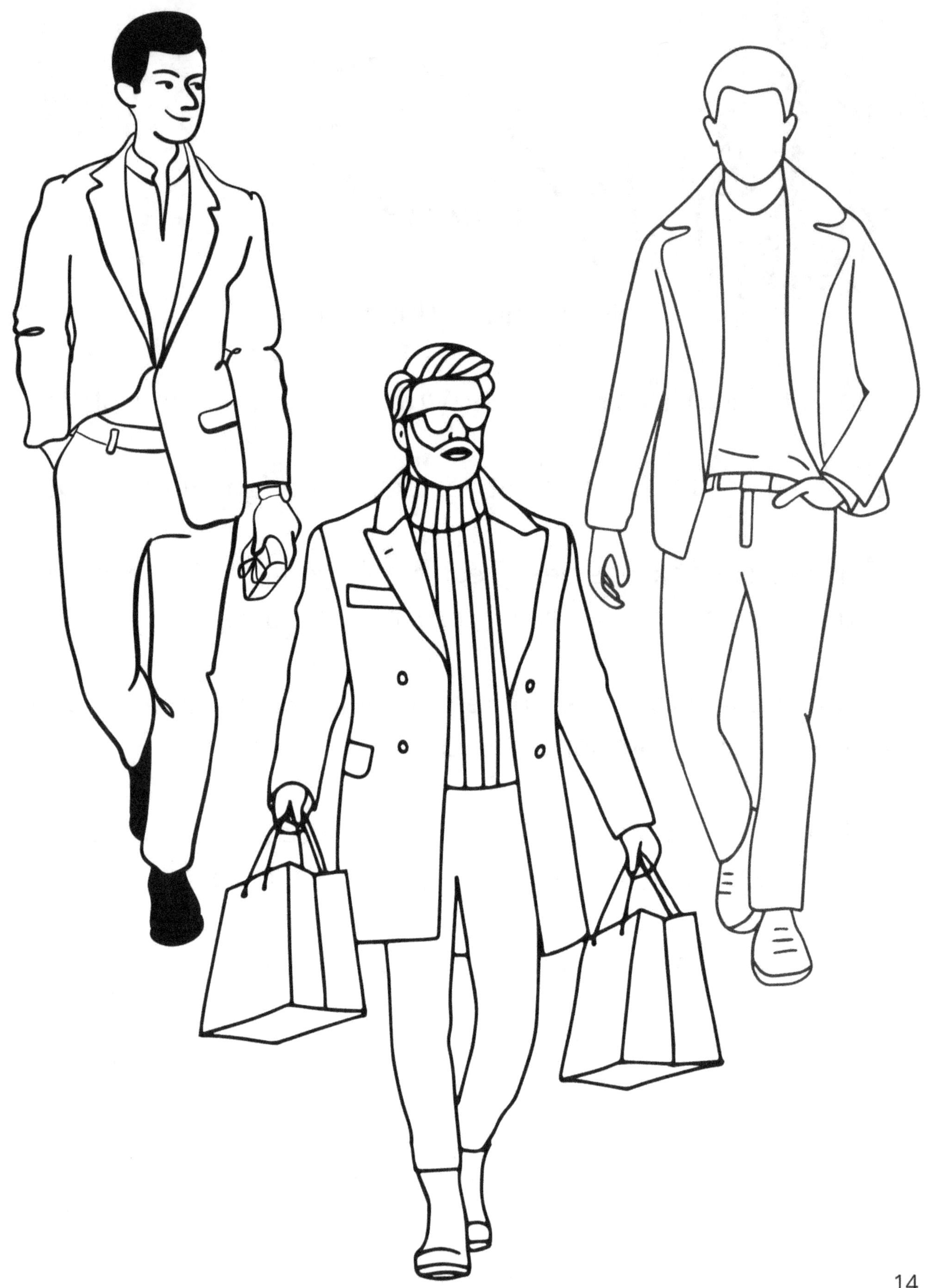

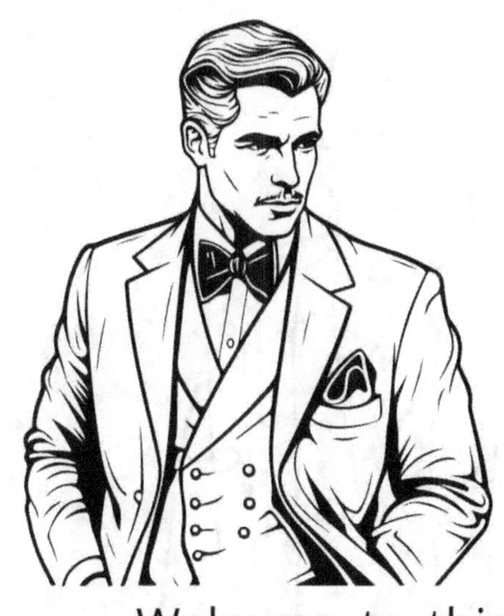

Author's Preface

Dear Reader,

Welcome to this creative journey into the world of men's fashion. This book was written with one purpose in mind: to give you a space where inspiration meets practice, and where each page can spark new ideas.

Inside, you'll find both guidance - with fundamentals of fashion and professional tips - and freedom, through male figure templates and sketching pages where you can experiment with limitless ideas.

Men's fashion is diverse: from minimalism to bold streetwear, from sharp tailoring to relaxed sportswear.

I hope these pages will inspire you to sketch, to try new things, and to see clothing as both function and art.

With passion and gratitude,

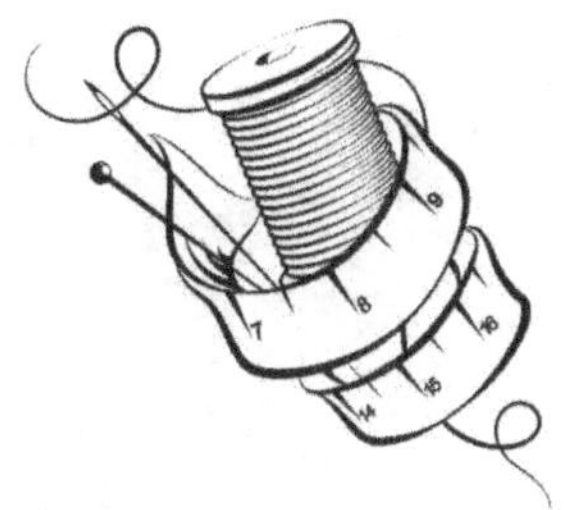

Niky Jadesson

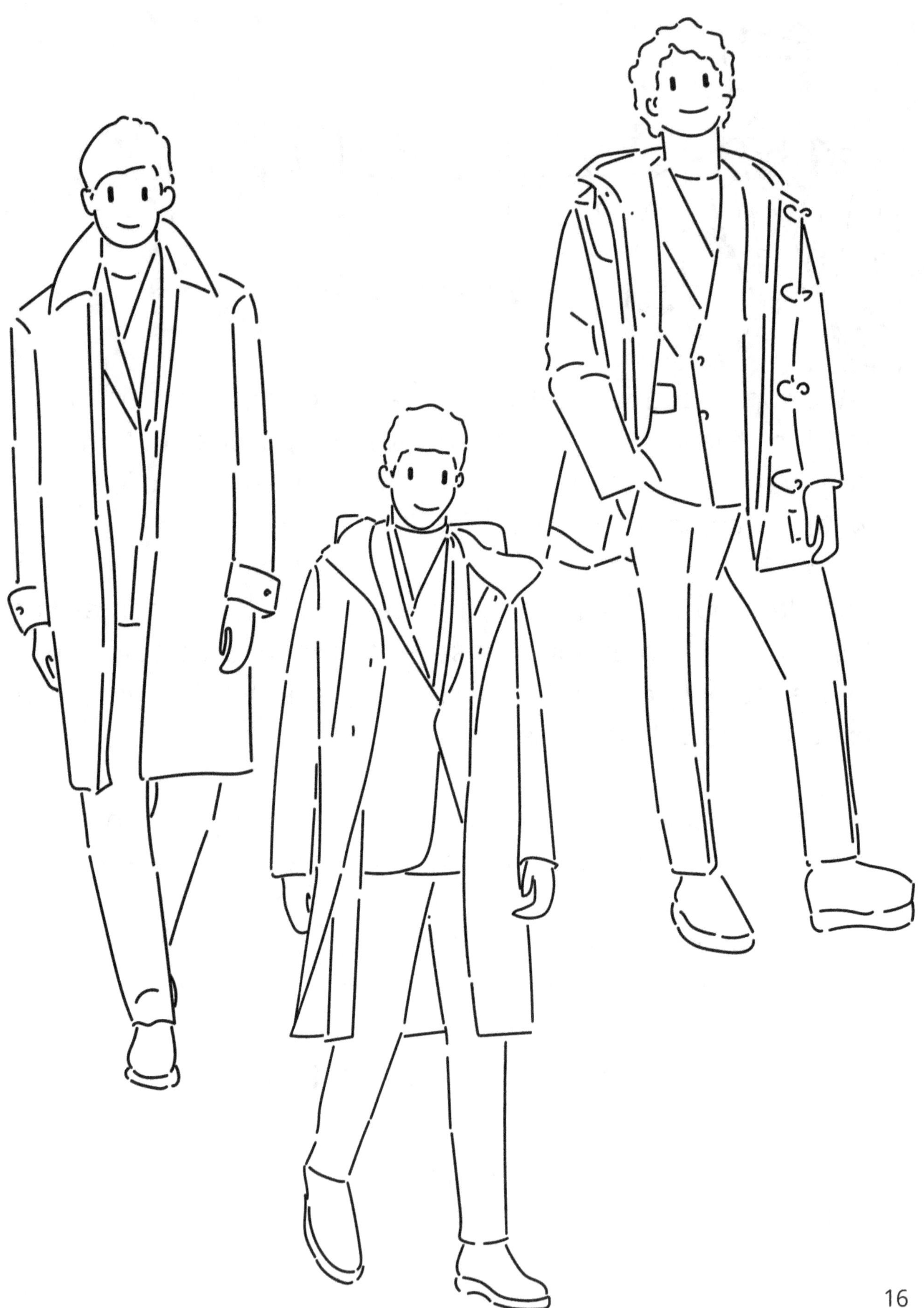

How to Use This Sketchbook

This sketchbook is both practical and creative. It gives you space to design outfits, explore styles, and reflect on your growth.

Here's how to get the most out of it:

- **Experiment Freely** – Try casual looks, formal tailoring, or bold streetwear. This is your playground for ideas.
- **Take Notes** – Write down fabrics, cuts, and accessories used for each design.
- **Use Templates** – The male figure silhouettes are guides to help you visualize clothing on the body.
- **Compare & Improve** – Track how your sketches evolve over time.
- **Repeat & Refine** – Don't be afraid to redraw outfits and explore variations.

Whether you're just beginning or aiming to refine your skills, this sketchbook is your personal design studio.

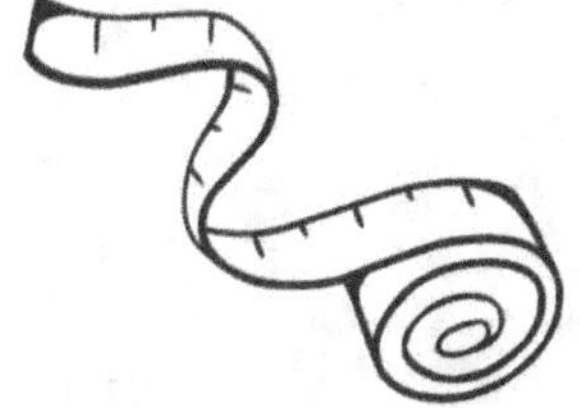

My Goals & Inspirations

Men's fashion is built on balance: structure and comfort, tradition and modernity. Before sketching, take a moment to define what kind of designer you want to be.

Questions to guide you:
- What type of menswear excites me most? (streetwear, formal wear, sportswear, casual)
- What story do I want my clothing to tell? (confidence, professionalism, rebellion, freedom)
- Who are my style icons? (classic designers, musicians, athletes, everyday men on the street)

Space for notes:
- My design goals: ______________________________
- My fashion inspirations: ____________________
- Fabrics or cuts I want to explore: ____________
- Skills I want to improve: __________________

Your goals don't have to be final - they can evolve just like fashion itself.

Tools & Materials
for Fashion Sketching

To sketch men's fashion, you'll need a few key tools. They help you translate your ideas into strong, clear designs:

- **Pencils & Erasers** – Use light strokes for jackets, shirts, and trousers before finalizing.
- **Fineliners** – Great for highlighting collars, cuffs, and tailoring seams.
- **Markers & Shading** – Neutral palettes (blacks, greys, blues) for suits, bold tones for streetwear.
- **Ruler & French Curves** – Helpful for the straight, structured lines often seen in men's clothing.
- **Digital Tablets** – Allow precise layering and editing, perfect for modern menswear design.
- **Fabric Samples** – Wool, denim, tweed, cotton - feeling these textures helps you sketch more realistically.

The right tools make the process smoother, but creativity always comes from you.

Tips
for Getting Started

Here are some ways to build confidence as you begin sketching:

- **Focus on Basics** – Practice shirts, trousers, and jackets before experimenting with complex outfits.
- **Study Tailoring** – Observe how seams shape a suit, how lapels add character, how cuffs or buttons complete the look.
- **Play with Proportions** – Slim-fit, oversized, relaxed - try them all.
- **Add Accessories** – Shoes, ties, hats, or bags can completely transform a design.
- **Consistency Wins** – Sketch a little every day instead of waiting for a "perfect" idea.

Men's fashion may seem simple, but its strength lies in the details. A single line can change an entire design.

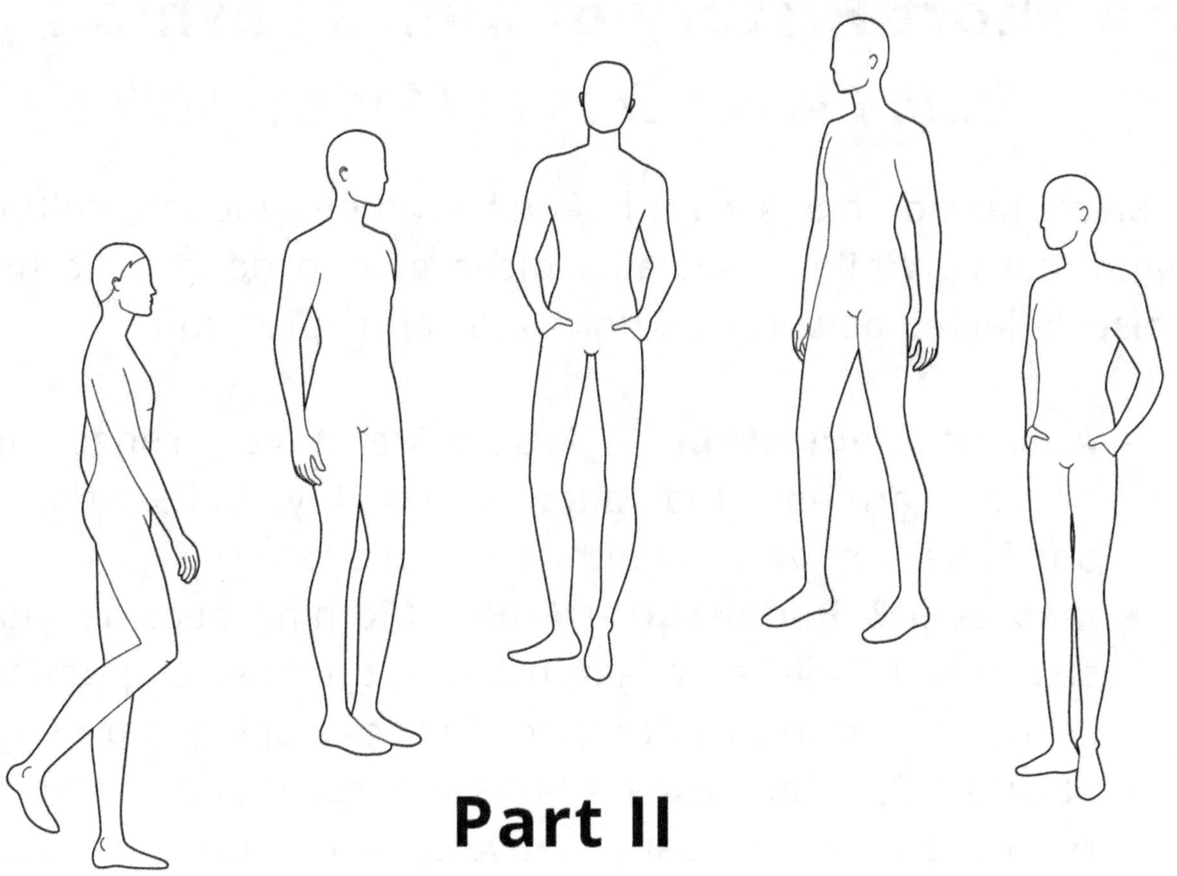

Part II
– Education & Fundamentals

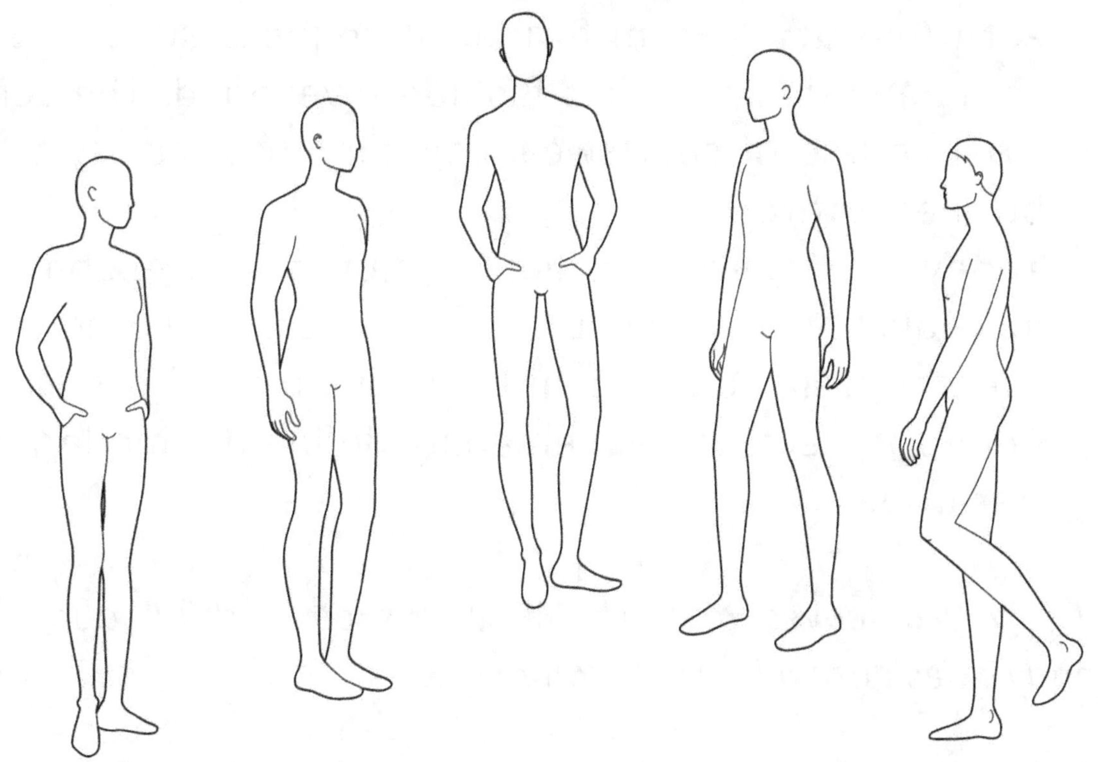

A Short History of Men's Fashion
– *From Classic Eras to Modern Styles*

Men's fashion has always been shaped by function, culture, and status. While practicality often guided design, clothing also reflected power, tradition, and self-expression.

- **Ancient Civilizations** – Men wore tunics, robes, and draped garments that allowed mobility. Belts, sandals, and jewelry showed wealth or social class.
- **Medieval & Renaissance Eras** – Clothing became more structured. Tailored coats, hose, and cloaks emphasized authority. Embroidery and rich fabrics displayed prestige.
- **18th & 19th Centuries** – Suits emerged as a symbol of refinement. Waistcoats, cravats, and fitted trousers became standard for gentlemen, while workwear evolved separately for labor and trade.
- **20th Century** – From formal three-piece suits to casual shirts and denim, men's fashion diversified. The century saw the rise of sportswear, military-inspired styles, and business attire.
- **Today** – Men's fashion embraces freedom and individuality. Minimalist streetwear, tailored suits, oversized silhouettes, and sustainable fabrics coexist. Comfort, identity, and versatility define the modern male wardrobe.

Every era leaves a mark. As you sketch, think about how today's designs will inspire tomorrow.

Male Silhouettes Through Time
– *Straight Cut, Slim, Relaxed, Oversized*

Silhouettes in men's fashion define both formality and lifestyle.

- **Straight Cut** – Classic, balanced, slightly boxy. A timeless foundation for suits and uniforms.
- **Slim Fit** – Narrow shoulders and tapered lines. Modern, sleek, and youthful.
- **Relaxed Fit** – Looser, comfortable cuts, often used in casualwear.
- **Oversized** – Dramatic proportions with exaggerated volume, common in streetwear and avant-garde looks.

Silhouettes are a silent language. Slim cuts feel sharp, oversized feels bold, relaxed feels approachable, while straight lines feel traditional.

When sketching, experiment with proportions. Small changes in shoulder width or pant taper can transform an entire design.

Color Theory in Men's Fashion
– *Matching, Contrasts & Seasonal Palettes*

Colors influence mood, style, and personality.

- **Neutral Foundations** – Shades like black, gray, navy, brown, and white dominate men's wardrobes because they are versatile and timeless.
- **Accent Colors** – Bold hues such as red, green, or mustard bring individuality without overwhelming the look.
- **Seasonal Palettes** –
  - *Spring*: light neutrals with pops of color.
  - *Summer*: cool blues, whites, and fresh tones.
  - *Autumn*: earthy browns, olives, deep oranges.
  - *Winter*: strong contrasts, like black with white, or dark tones with metallic accents.
- **Color Psychology** – Dark tones create formality, light tones suggest ease, and bright tones add confidence.

A single accent-like a colorful tie, jacket lining, or sneakers-can completely shift a simple outfit.

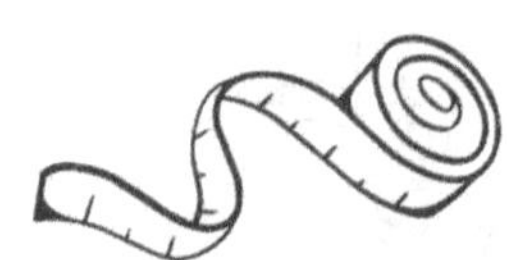
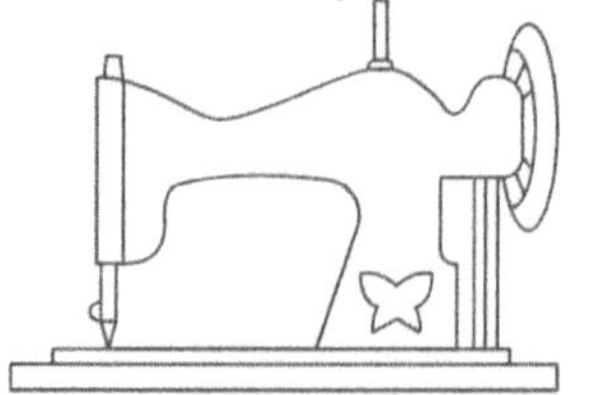

Fabrics & Textures for Men's Clothing
– *Wool, Cotton, Denim, Leather*

Fabric determines comfort, durability, and style.

- **Wool** – Warm, structured, and perfect for suits, coats, and knitwear.
- **Cotton** – Breathable, versatile, and widely used for shirts, trousers, and casualwear.
- **Denim** – Rugged, practical, and iconic in men's fashion. A symbol of casual strength.
- **Leather** – Strong, long-lasting, often used for jackets, shoes, and accessories.

Texture tells as much of a story as silhouette. Smooth fabrics look formal, while rough fabrics look casual.

Try sketching the same jacket in wool and leather-you'll see how the mood changes instantly.

Fashion Sketching Tools

– Pencils, Markers, Digital Options

Your tools help capture the masculine form and structure of designs.

- **Graphite Pencils** – Great for sharp outlines, shading, and structured lines.
- **Markers** – Add strong blocks of color, ideal for bold masculine palettes.
- **Colored Pencils** – Layer subtle tones and shading for fabric effects.
- **Inks & Pens** – Create sharp, defined contours.
- **Digital Tools** – Tablets make experimenting with proportions and textures fast and versatile.

The best tool is the one you'll actually use consistently. Start simple, grow with practice.

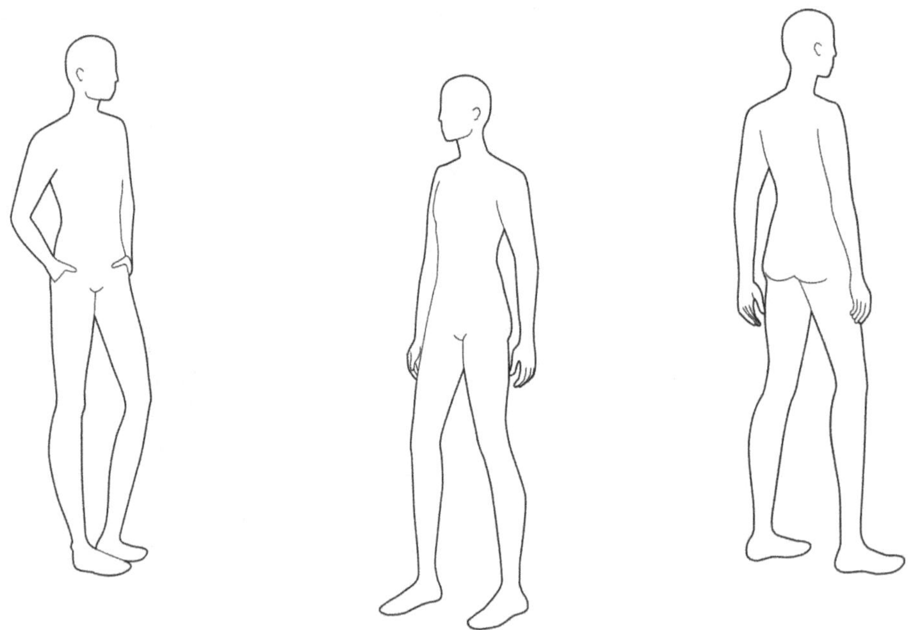

Step-by-Step:

Casual Day Outfit (T-shirt, Shirt, Jeans)

Casualwear is about ease, comfort, and individuality.

1. **Start with the Silhouette** – Straight or relaxed cut for comfort.

2. **Outline Basics** – A T-shirt, open shirt, or jeans.

3. **Add Functional Details** – Pockets, stitching, zippers, or rolled sleeves.

4. **Color Palette** – Neutral shades with subtle accents (gray, white, light blue, olive).

5. **Texture Effects** – Show denim's roughness, cotton's softness, or layered fabrics.

Casual designs should look effortless-something that feels natural to wear every day.

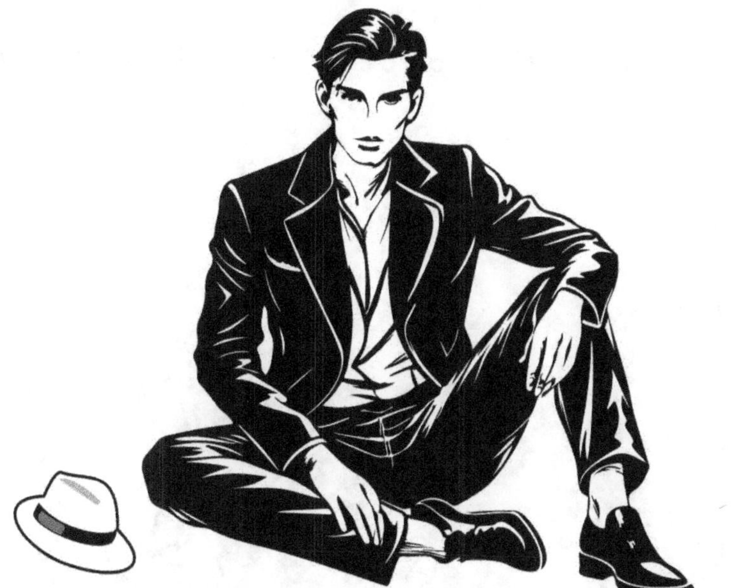

Step-by-Step:

Evening Look (Suit, Jacket, Formalwear)

Eveningwear for men blends sophistication with personality.

1. **Silhouette** – Choose slim or straight cut, depending on style.

2. **Jacket Details** – Lapels, buttons, vents, and length define character.

3. **Trousers** – Match the jacket in fabric, but adjust cut for comfort.

4. **Shirt & Accessories** – Collars, ties, cufflinks, belts, or shoes complete the look.

5. **Colors & Fabrics** – Dark tones like navy or charcoal for elegance; lighter shades for modern flair.

A formal look should inspire confidence while staying true to the wearer's character.

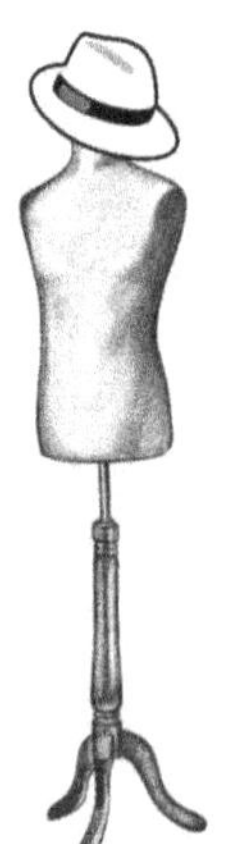

Common Design Mistakes in Men's Fashion

(and How to Avoid Them)

Mistakes happen, but awareness helps prevent them.

- **Poor Proportions** – Shoulders too wide or trousers too long disrupt balance.
- **Excessive Details** – Too many zippers, seams, or layers can overwhelm.
- **Color Clashes** – Loud combinations may look unpolished.
- **Ignoring Fabric Functionality** – Heavy fabrics for summer or light fabrics for coats don't work.
- **One-Size-Fits-All Thinking** – Men's bodies vary greatly; designs should adapt.

The strongest designs balance style, function, and fit.

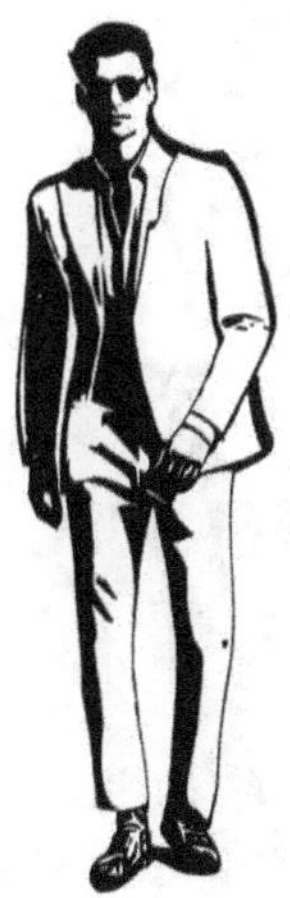

Tips & Tricks for Men's Fashion Designers

- Use layering to add depth and versatility.

- Focus on fit: even a simple shirt can look extraordinary when well cut.

- Neutral palettes can become exciting with textures- try mixing wool with cotton or denim.

- Sketch accessories too: belts, hats, shoes, and bags complete the outfit.

- Practice sketching different age groups and body types for versatility.

Men's fashion thrives on subtlety-small changes in line, fabric, or cut can create big impact.

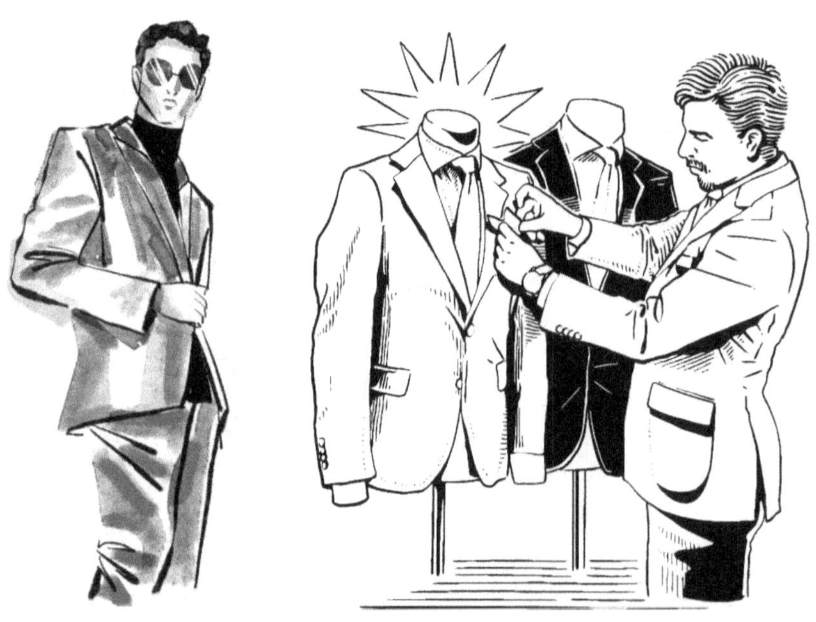

Step-by-Step Guide
to This Sketchbook

This sketchbook is your training ground for men's fashion design.

- **Practice Silhouettes** – Use templates to test proportions and fits.
- **Experiment with Fabrics** – Shade or color to represent wool, cotton, denim, or leather.
- **Play with Color** – Try neutral bases with unexpected accents.
- **Think in Collections** – Design casual, formal, and streetwear sets that share a theme.
- **Use Notes & Reflections** – Write what inspired you, what worked, and what you'd refine.

By the last page, you'll have a personal collection of masculine designs that reflect your creative evolution.

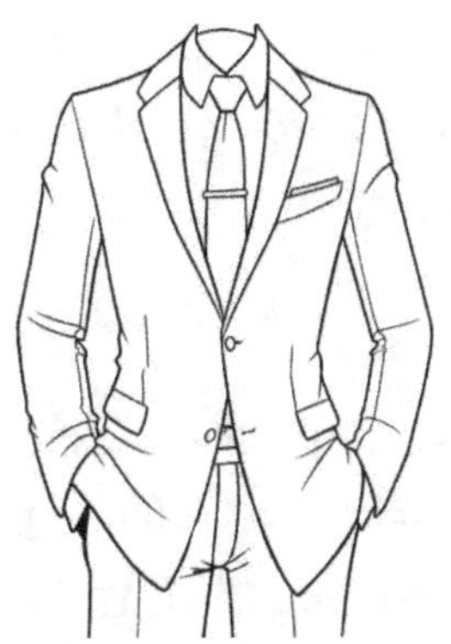

Fashion Sketching Fundamentals:
Step by Step

Men's fashion sketching has its own characteristics, focusing on structure, balance, and proportion. While men's silhouettes are often straighter than women's, creative design allows for experimentation. Follow this process as a guide:

Step 1: Construct the Base Silhouette
- Sketch guidelines for shoulders, chest, waist, hips, and legs.
- Male proportions are usually broader in the shoulders and straighter in the torso.

Step 2: Outline the Core Outfit
- Use geometric forms to represent basic garments: rectangles for shirts, tapered shapes for trousers, or structured blocks for jackets.
- Keep the sketch simple and clean before adding detail.

Step 3: Add Garment Features
- Introduce collars, cuffs, buttons, zippers, seams, and pockets.
- These small details often define whether a look is casual, business, or sporty.

Step 4: Suggest Fabrics & Textures
- Straight, even lines → denim or cotton.
- Heavy shading → wool or leather.
- Cross-hatching → tweed or structured fabrics.

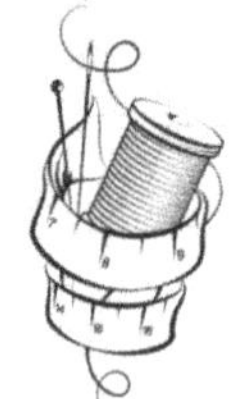

Step 5: Apply Color & Tone
- Men's fashion often uses muted or monochrome palettes, but don't be afraid of experimenting with bold colors.
- Use shadows to show fabric folds and layering.

Step 6: Finalize the Sketch
- Strengthen the outlines and adjust proportions.
- Add side notes: type of fabric, season, or styling inspiration.

Men's fashion sketching rewards precision, but don't let that limit your creativity. Use these steps as a flexible framework.

Mini Exercise:
Sketch a simple shirt-and-trousers combo twice: first as a casual weekend outfit (soft cotton shirt + sneakers), then as a formal outfit (structured dress shirt + leather shoes). Compare how posture and detail affect the overall mood.

QUICK & EASY EVERYDAY FASHION LOOK

Every day, men's fashion is about functionality and style blended together. This exercise will help you create a simple look that feels natural yet sharp.

5 Steps to Design a Casual Men's Look:

1. Draw a relaxed male silhouette, shoulders slightly broad.

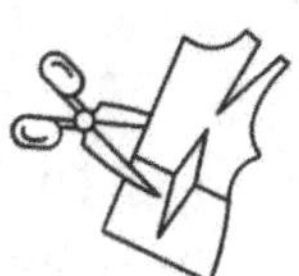

2. Add a basic t-shirt or casual shirt.

3. Pair it with chinos or denim trousers.

4. Suggest everyday shoes – sneakers, loafers, or casual boots.

5. Include subtle accessories like a watch, a backpack, or a belt.

Styling Notes:

- Neutral palettes (gray, navy, white, black) dominate everyday men's fashion.
- Small variations like rolled-up sleeves, untucked shirts, or layered jackets add personality.
- Fabrics such as cotton, denim, and jersey are comfortable yet versatile.

Why Practice This?

Casual men's looks are perfect for practicing balance and proportion. These sketches also help you get comfortable with layering, posture, and subtle detailing.

Reflection Prompt:

- How does the outfit change if you swap chinos for ripped jeans?
- What mood does each version of the look communicate?

Try sketching your own "go-to" everyday outfit on this page. Experiment with small details to see how they shift the style from simple to stylish.

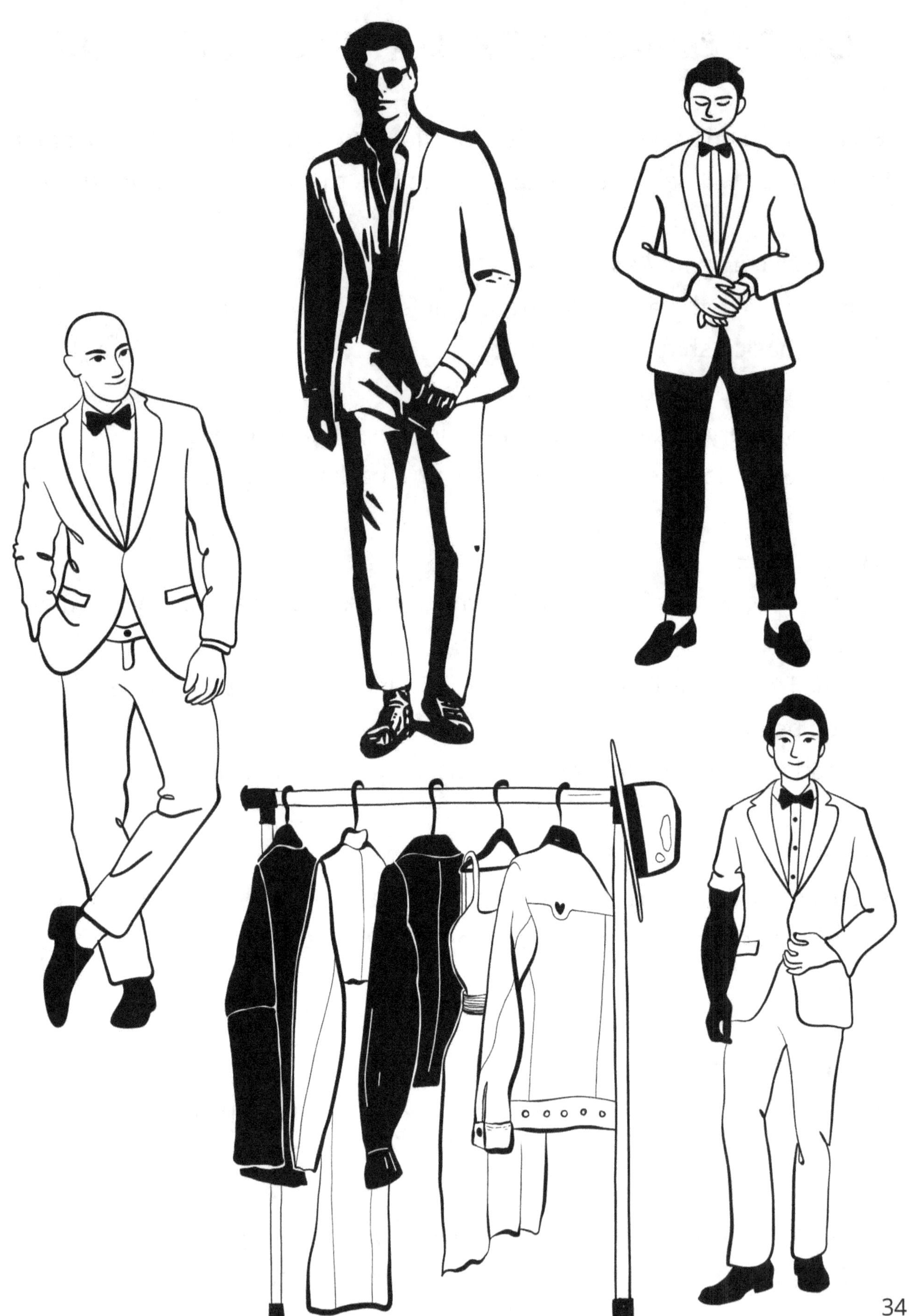

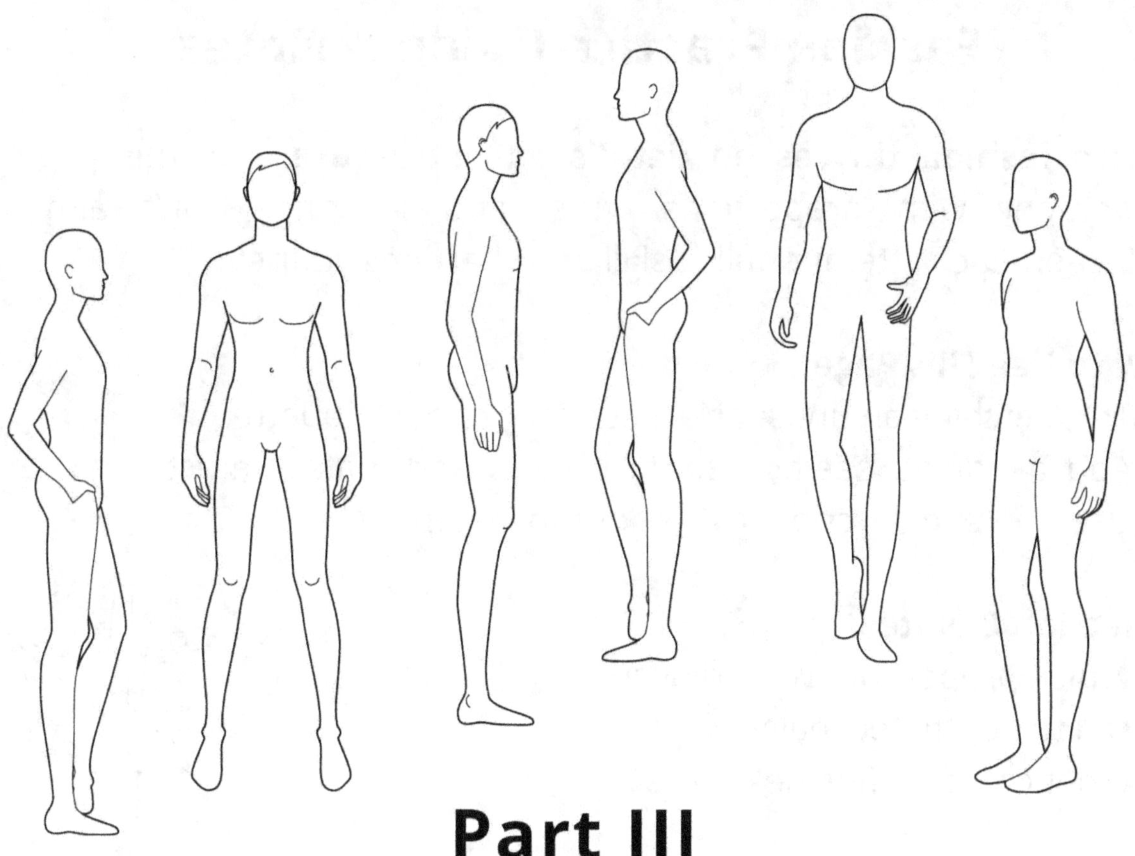

Part III
– Sketchbook & Practice

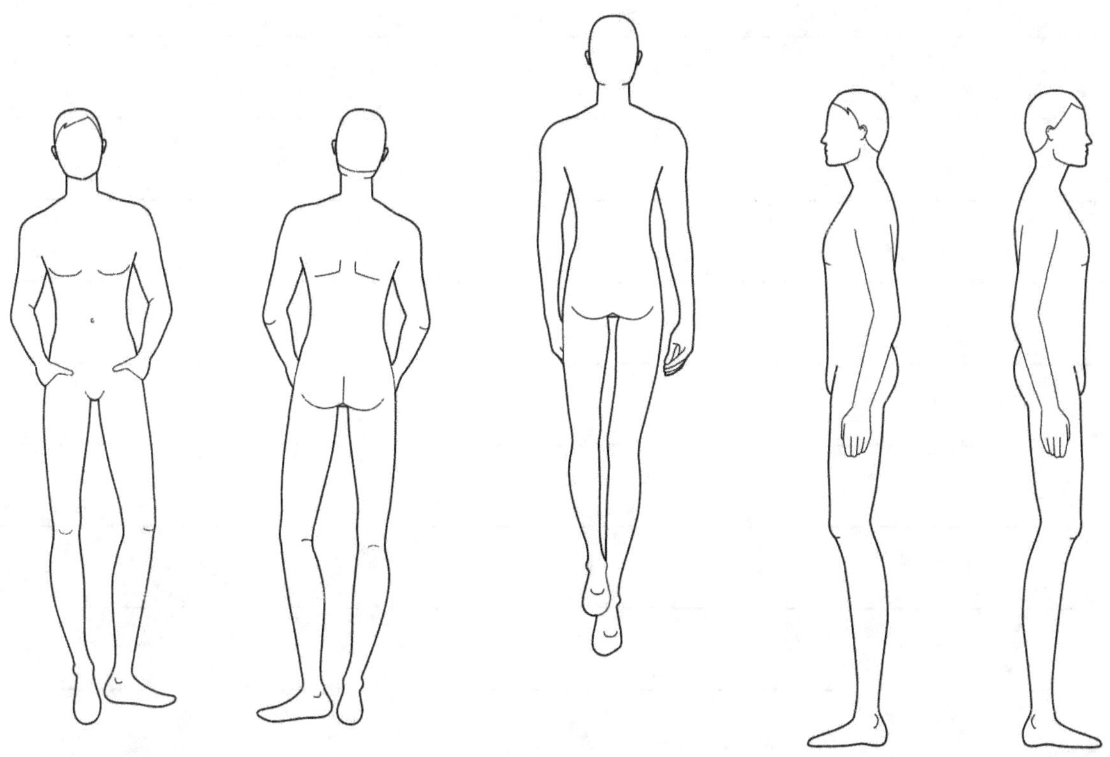

Fashion Practice Guide & Notes

Men's fashion thrives on details and structure. Use this page to experiment with proportions, cuts, and layering. Don't aim for perfection-each attempt builds skill and sharpens your eye.

How to Use This Page:
- Try sketching an unusual jacket cut or pant silhouette.
- Add layering to see how shirts, blazers, and coats interact.
- Use notes to describe texture or movement.

Reflection & Notes:
- Which proportion worked best?
- Did the outfit feel balanced?
- What could I refine next time?

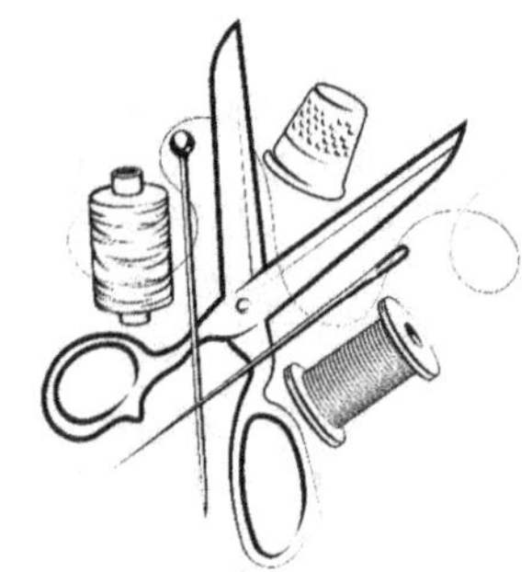

Pro Tip: *Precision in detail defines great men's fashion.*

Outfit Inspiration: Streetwear

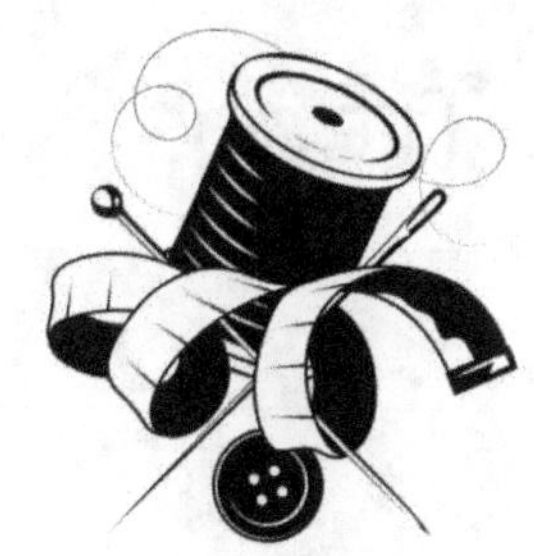

Classic Streetwear

Classic streetwear is all about timeless staples that never lose their cool factor. Imagine straight-leg jeans in a medium wash, paired with a crisp white t-shirt that feels both casual and intentional. Layer a bomber jacket or a varsity-style jacket over it to add that instant urban touch. Sneakers, preferably low-profile in neutral colors, finish the look.

Accessories are kept simple – maybe a baseball cap or a minimal watch. The strength of this style lies in its versatility: it works on a relaxed day in the city, at a casual social event, or even styled up with sharper cuts for evening wear.

This look is a reminder that you don't need to overcomplicate fashion. By focusing on well-fitting, quality basics, the outfit becomes timeless.

Pro Tip: *Stick to neutral shades like black, white, grey, or navy for the foundation. Then add just one bold accent – maybe a red jacket, a graphic tee, or brightly colored sneakers – to create a focal point without overpowering the look.*

Trends

Inspiration

Textiles

Notes

Details

Swatches

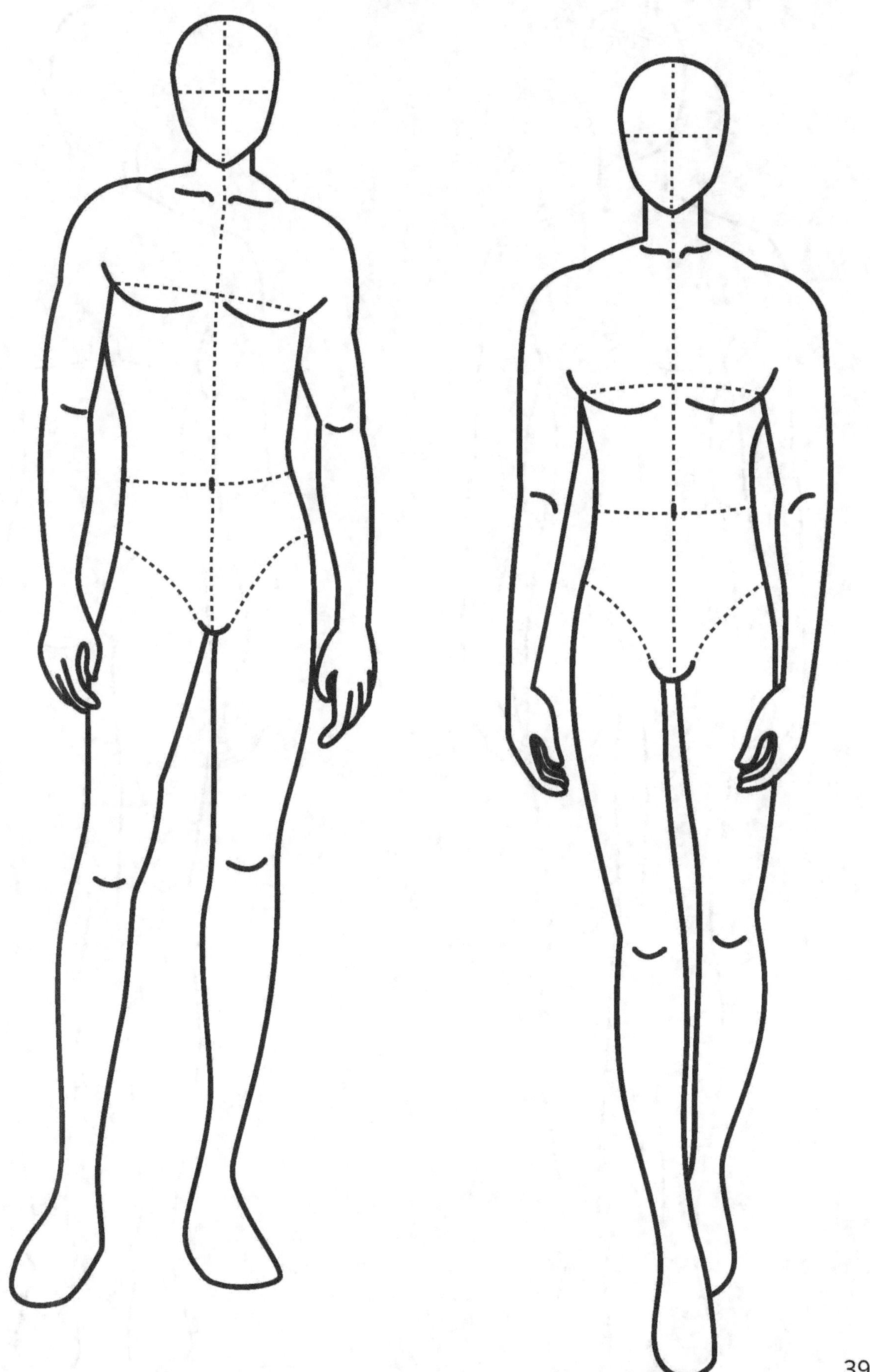

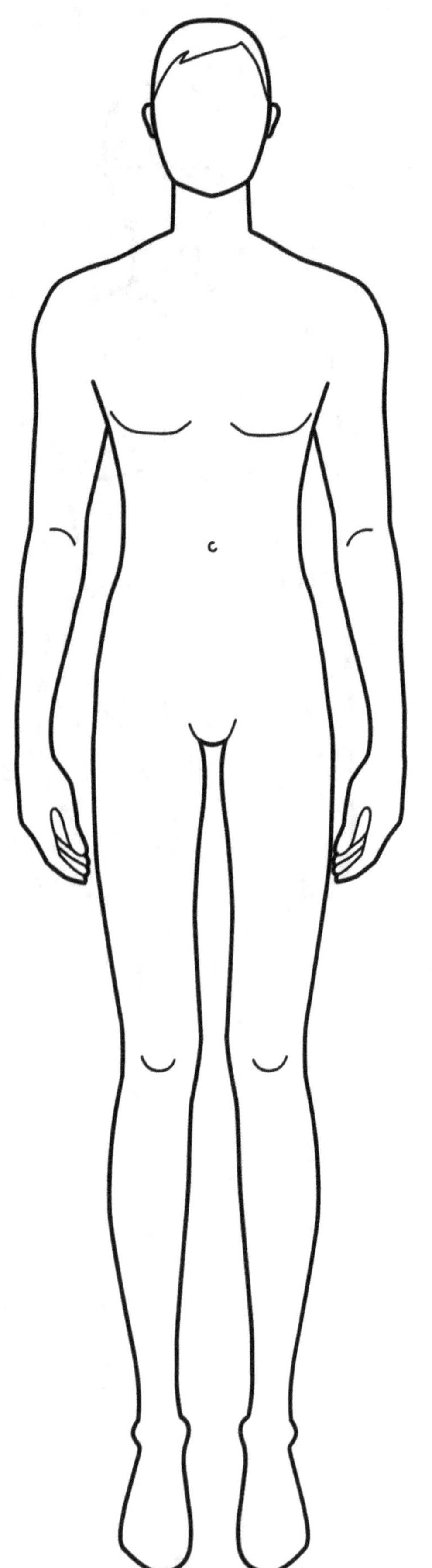
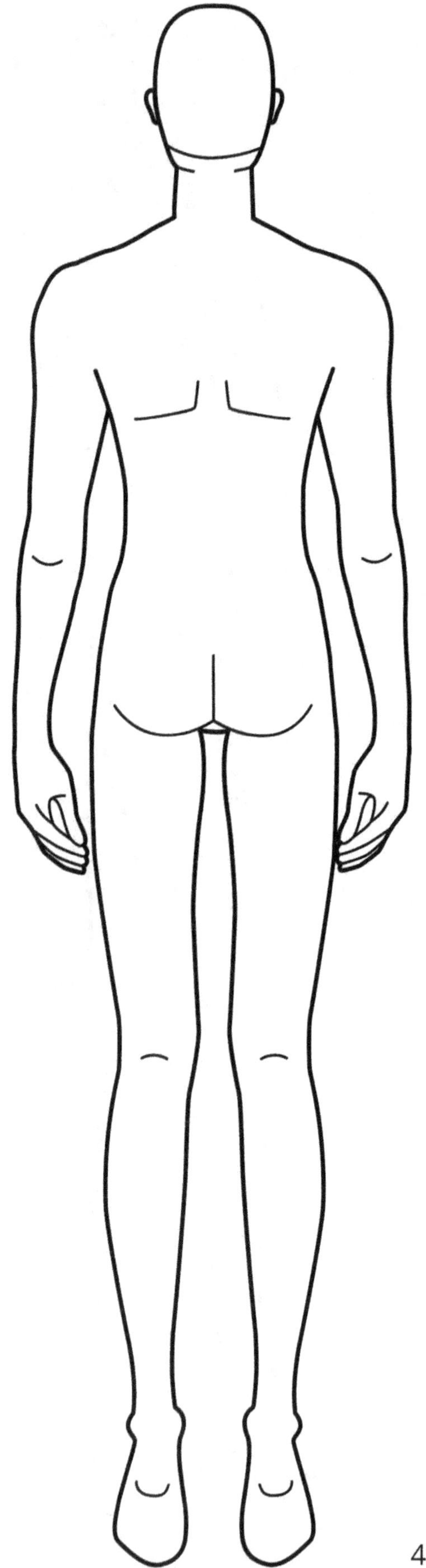

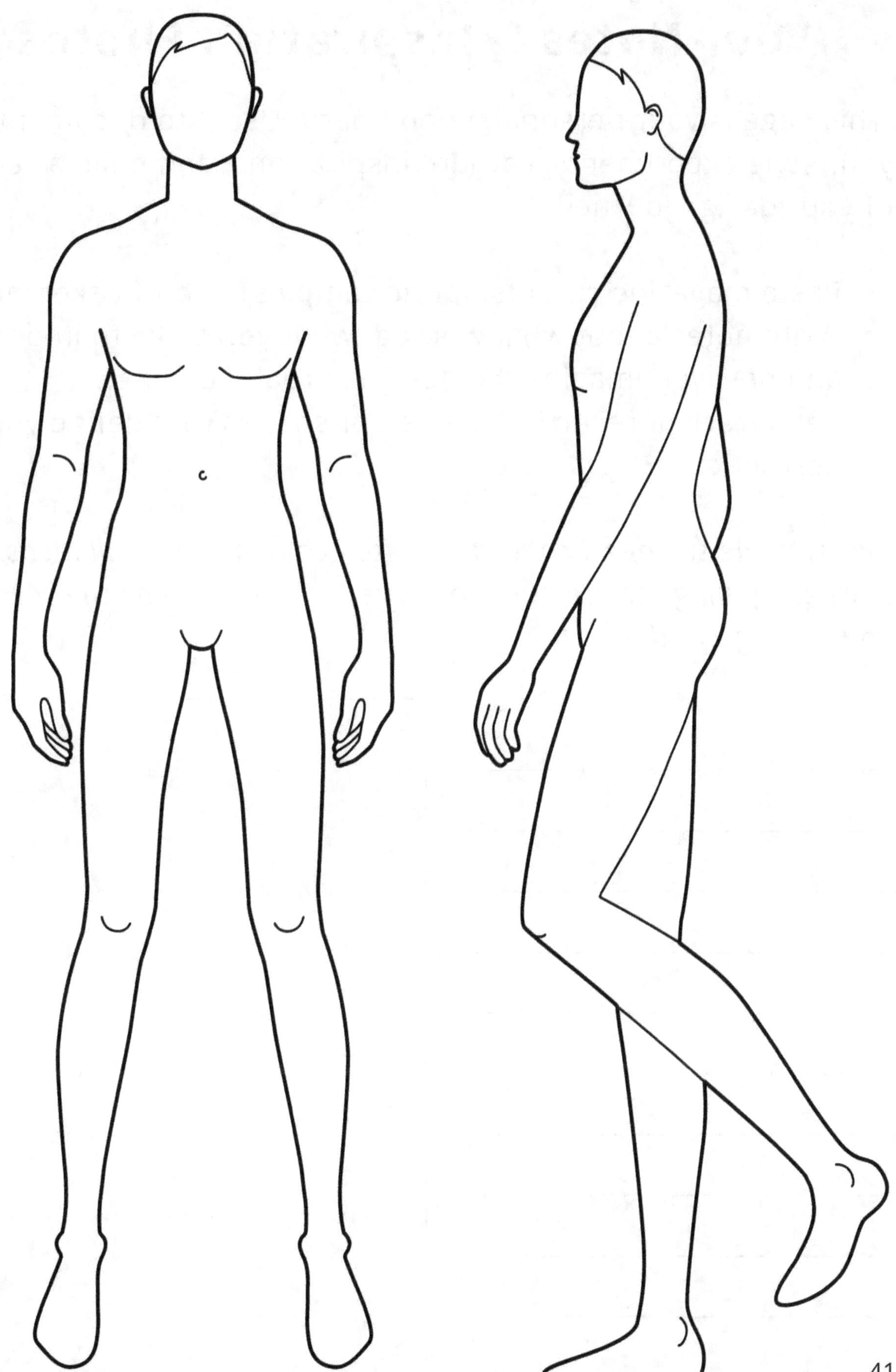

Your Notes & Inspiration Photos

This page is your personal mood board. Use it to document your style experiments, capture inspirations, and build a record of your design journey.

- Paste magazine cutouts, fabric samples, or outfit sketches.
- Write notes about what worked, what you'd like to improve, and how you imagine the design in real life.
- Keep track of recurring themes or shapes that define your aesthetic.

Pro Tip: The strongest collections often come from small ideas. Save everything that catches your eye – it may become the seed of your next great design.

Outfit Inspiration:
Office Chic and Runway Glam

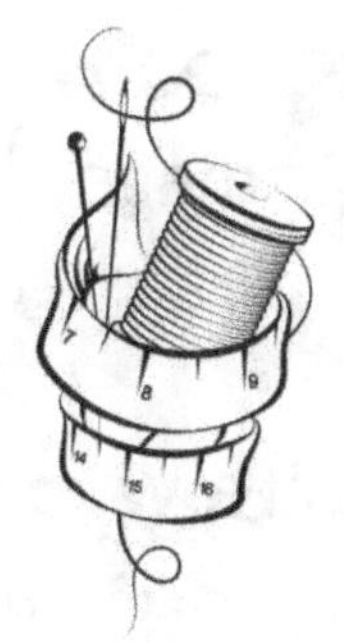

Classic Business Suit + Red Carpet Tuxedo

Office Chic Inspiration

The timeless business suit is a foundation of men's office style. A tailored navy or charcoal suit, paired with a crisp white shirt and a simple tie, creates a look of authority. Polished oxford shoes and a leather briefcase reinforce professionalism. Subtle details such as cufflinks or a pocket square add refinement without excess.

Runway Glam Inspiration

Nothing says red carpet like a perfectly cut tuxedo. Black remains a staple, but deep jewel tones or velvet fabrics elevate the drama. Pair with patent leather shoes and a bow tie for a classic finish. Slim cuts bring a modern feel, while double-breasted designs nod to timeless elegance.

Fashion Practice Guide & Notes

Quick sketches keep ideas fresh. Don't hesitate-capture the first image that comes to mind, even if it's rough. Fast work often leads to unexpected originality.

How to Use This Page:
- Do a 5-minute warm-up sketch.
- Focus on one piece: shirt, trousers, or shoes.
- Annotate fabric choice and styling notes.

Reflection & Notes:
- Did speed help me simplify?
- Which element feels strongest?
- What would I refine next time?

Pro Tip: *Speed sketching improves clarity and sharpens instincts.*

____

____

____

____

____

____

____

____

Outfit Inspiration: Streetwear

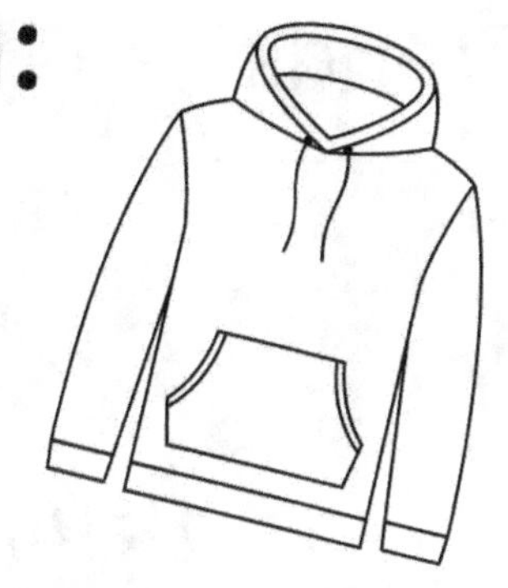

Sport-Inspired Streetwear

At the intersection of athletic wear and urban cool sits sport-inspired streetwear. Think joggers with elastic cuffs, sleek trainers, oversized hoodies, and baseball caps. This look takes inspiration from the track and gym but translates it into everyday wear. Layering is key here – a bomber over a hoodie, or a zip-up jacket with bold side stripes, can instantly elevate the aesthetic. The appeal of this style lies in movement and comfort: it's easy to wear yet still sharp when styled well.

Colors often echo sports uniforms – blacks, whites, reds, and bold color-blocking. This style thrives on active energy, perfect for someone who wants fashion that can keep up with their lifestyle.

Pro Tip: *Match your sneakers to one piece in the outfit – whether it's the hoodie, a stripe on the pants, or even a hat. That small detail creates cohesion and makes the outfit look intentional, not accidental.*

Trends

Inspiration

Textiles

Notes

Details

Swatches

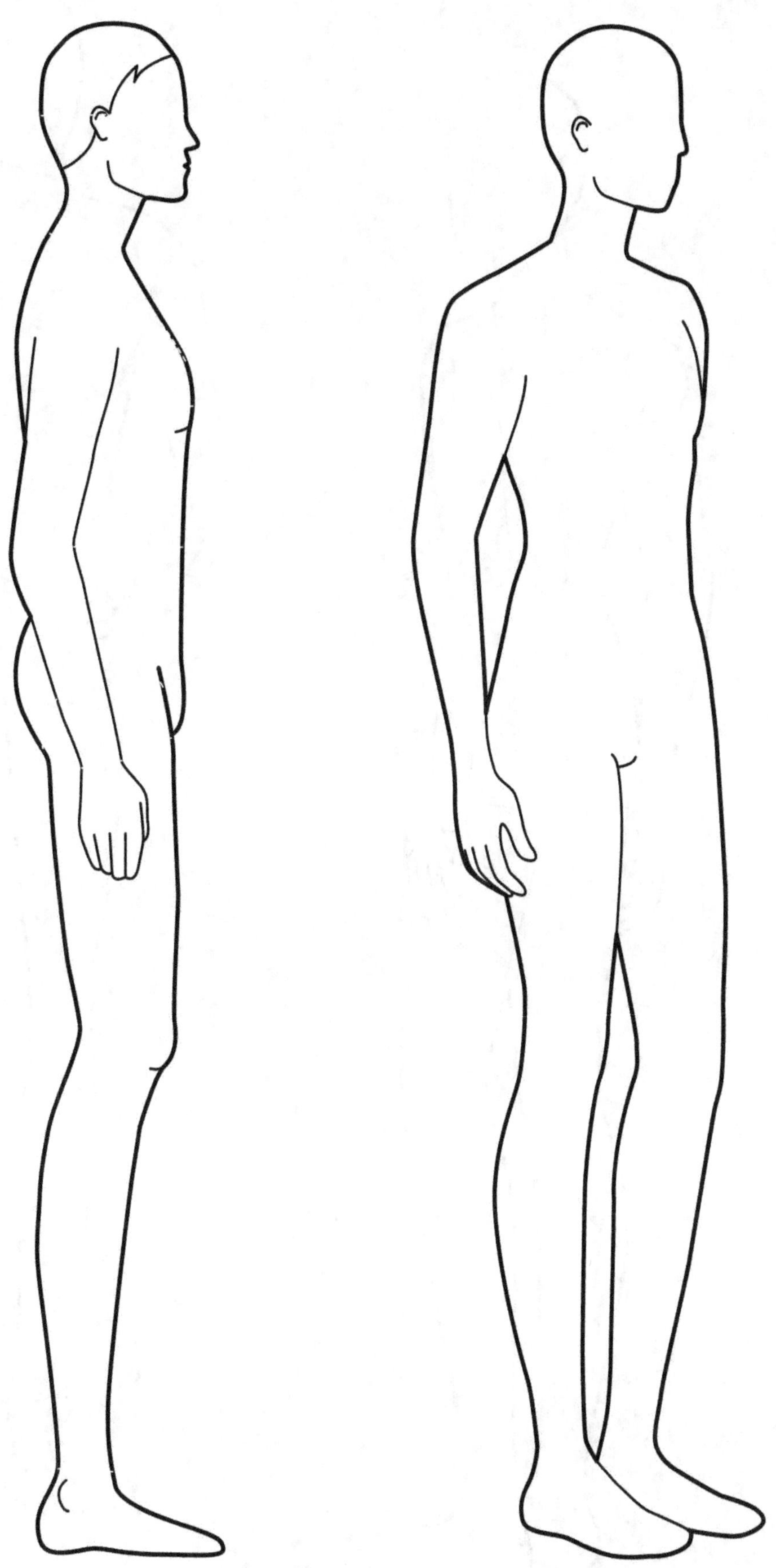

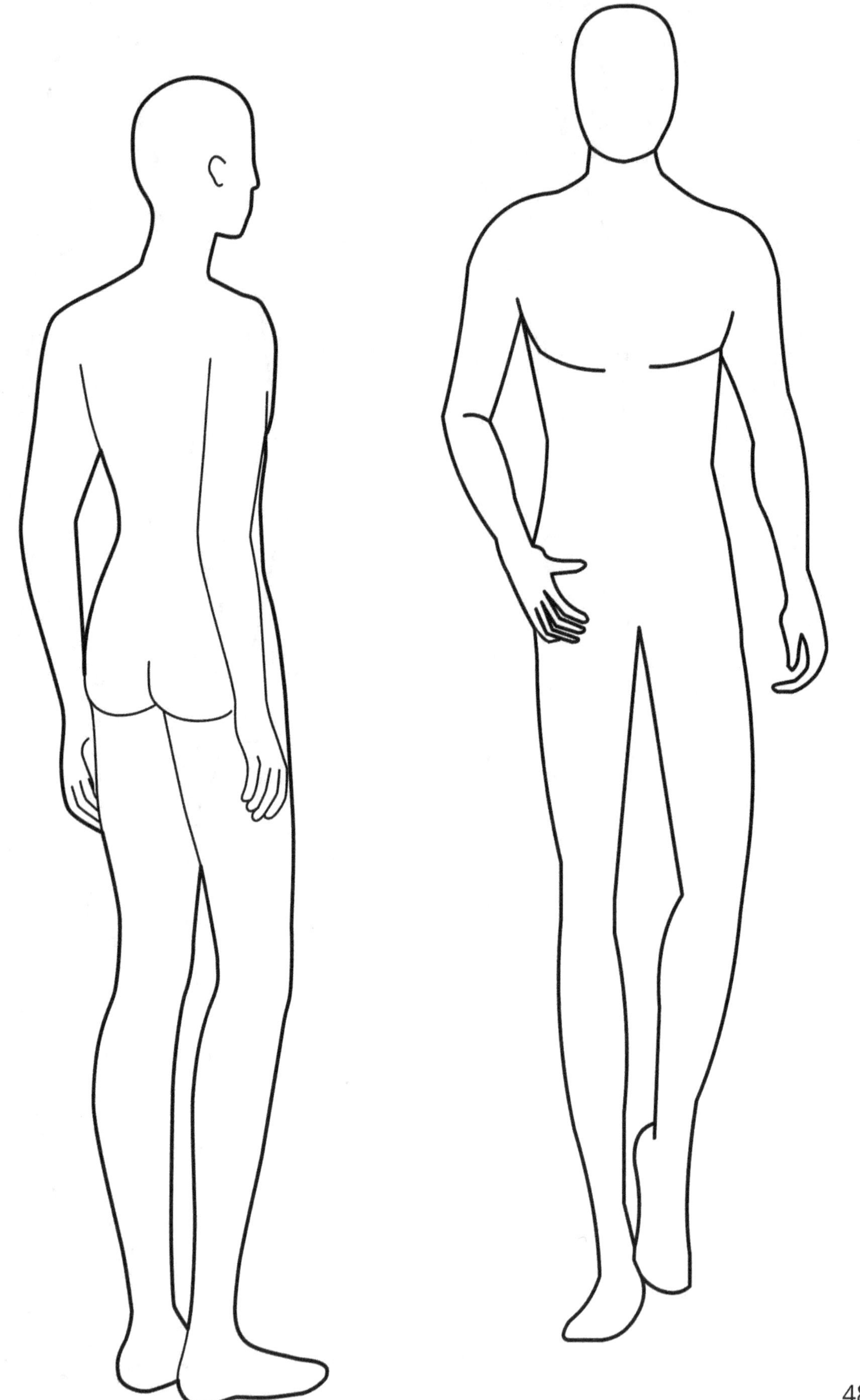

Your Notes & Inspiration Photos

This page is your personal mood board. Use it to document your style experiments, capture inspirations, and build a record of your design journey.

- Paste magazine cutouts, fabric samples, or outfit sketches.
- Write notes about what worked, what you'd like to improve, and how you imagine the design in real life.
- Keep track of recurring themes or shapes that define your aesthetic.

Pro Tip: *The strongest collections often come from small ideas. Save everything that catches your eye – it may become the seed of your next great design.*

Outfit Inspiration: Office Chic and Runway Glam

Minimalist Workwear + Futuristic Menswear

Office Chic Inspiration

Minimalism in men's office wear thrives on clean lines and muted palettes. Pair slim-fit trousers with a lightweight sweater or crisp shirt in solid colors. Shoes should remain sleek – loafers or leather sneakers maintain polish without excess formality. This look communicates focus, simplicity, and modern professionalism.

Runway Glam Inspiration

Futuristic menswear is bold and experimental. Think metallic fabrics, sculptural outerwear, or sharp asymmetrical tailoring. Silver, chrome, or holographic accents create an otherworldly effect. Footwear may feature unconventional materials, blending fashion with innovation.

Fashion Practice Guide & Notes

Clothing communicates character. Use this page to design an outfit inspired by a lifestyle, mood, or situation.

How to Use This Page:
- Pick a theme (sports, travel, urban life).
- Express it through cuts, accessories, and fabrics.
- Write how each detail supports the theme.

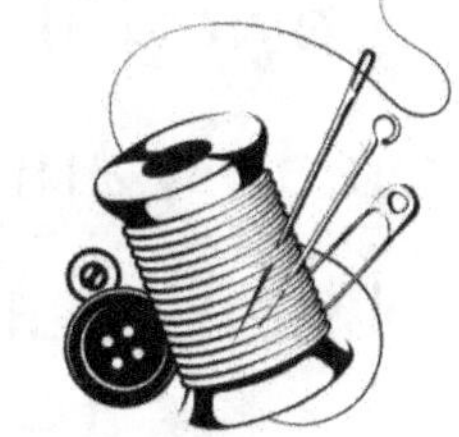

Reflection & Notes:
- Did I capture the chosen mood?
- Which part of the outfit tells the story best?
- How could I push the concept further?

Pro Tip: *Men's style becomes powerful when it reflects identity.*

____

____

____

____

____

____

____

____

Outfit Inspiration: Streetwear

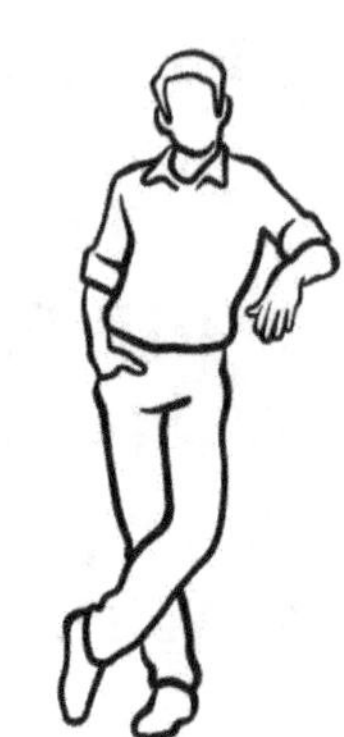

Oversized & Relaxed

Oversized streetwear is rooted in comfort but creates a powerful statement. Picture a slouchy hoodie, extra-wide jeans, and chunky sneakers. Add in a bucket hat or oversized beanie, and suddenly the outfit feels street-smart and trend-driven. The oversized silhouette has been embraced by younger generations as a way to reject formality and prioritize ease.

However, this isn't just about baggy clothing. The proportions must be thought through – pairing extremely wide pants with an oversized top can drown the figure, so many choose one oversized piece balanced with something slimmer. Oversized outfits give room for movement and self-expression, and they feel especially modern when styled with layers or bold accessories.

Pro Tip: *Focus on proportion play. If your hoodie is extremely oversized, balance it with more fitted joggers. If your pants are wide, pair them with a cropped or slightly slimmer jacket. This keeps the look edgy but wearable.*

Trends

Inspiration

Textiles

Notes

Details

Swatches

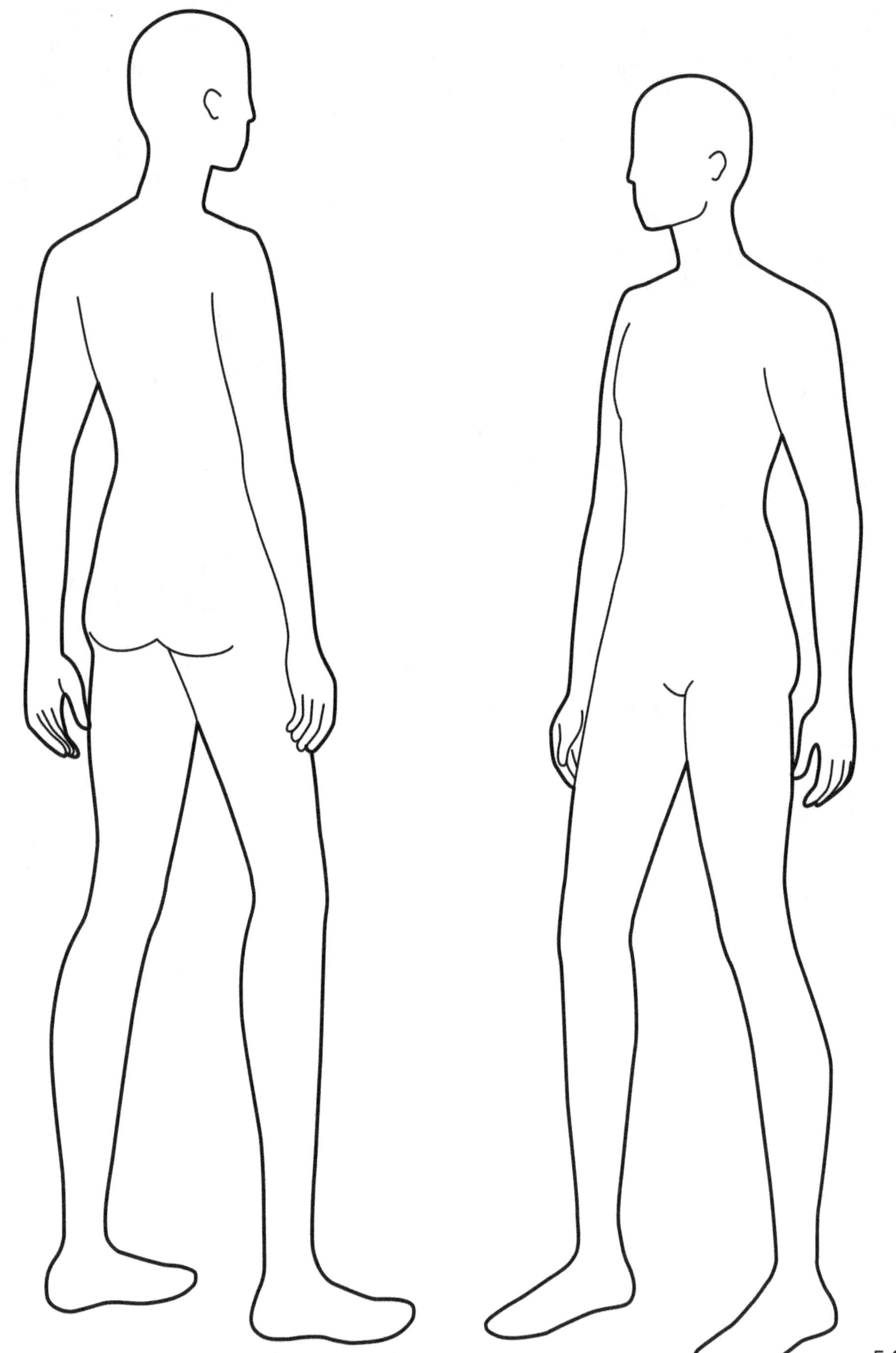

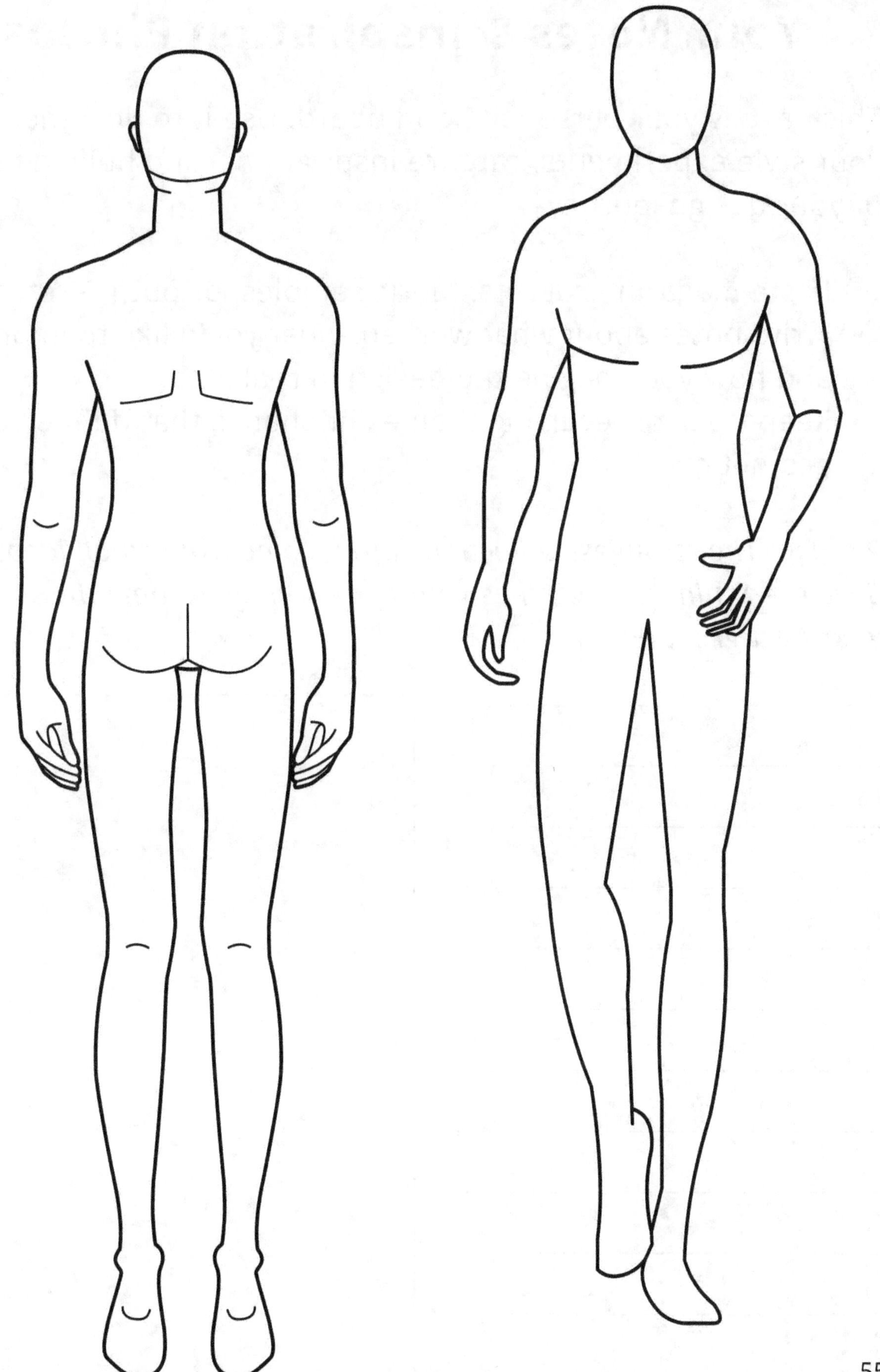

Your Notes & Inspiration Photos

This page is your personal mood board. Use it to document your style experiments, capture inspirations, and build a record of your design journey.

- Paste magazine cutouts, fabric samples, or outfit sketches.
- Write notes about what worked, what you'd like to improve, and how you imagine the design in real life.
- Keep track of recurring themes or shapes that define your aesthetic.

Pro Tip*: The strongest collections often come from small ideas. Save everything that catches your eye – it may become the seed of your next great design.*

Outfit Inspiration:
Office Chic and Runway Glam

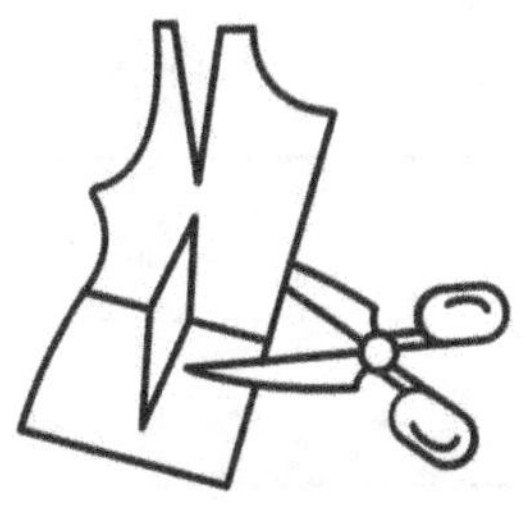

Creative Professional + Festival Glam

Office Chic Inspiration

In creative industries, men can embrace expressive office looks. Patterned shirts, relaxed blazers, or trousers in unexpected shades bring personality into the workplace. Layering lightweight scarves or textured knits adds individuality without losing professionalism.

Runway Glam Inspiration

Festival-inspired glam is energetic and eclectic. Sequined jackets, embellished denim, and bold prints dominate. Fringe, embroidery, and metallic accessories enhance the celebratory spirit. These looks thrive under lights, radiating confidence and vibrancy.

Fashion Practice Guide & Notes

Innovation starts with contrast. This page is your lab for mixing different style codes and testing boundaries.

How to Use This Page:
- Combine casual and formal (hoodie with blazer).
- Experiment with oversized vs. tailored fits.
- Note what clashes and what complements.

Reflection & Notes:
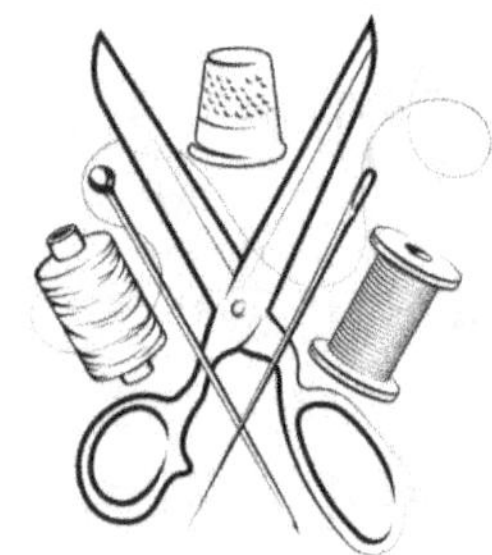
- Which combo surprised me most?
- Did the mix feel balanced or chaotic?
- Would this design work in real life?

Pro Tip: *Unexpected blends often create fresh men's looks.*

Outfit Inspiration: Streetwear

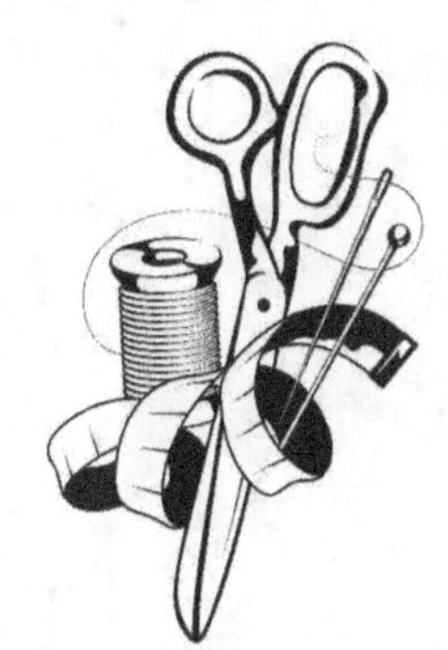

Denim Street Style

Denim has been a streetwear staple for decades, and the key is variety. Ripped jeans, distressed jackets, patchwork designs, and mixed washes keep the look fresh and experimental. Layering denim over graphic tees or hoodies gives a gritty yet stylish vibe. This style celebrates the "lived-in" aesthetic – the more unique and worn a piece looks, the cooler it feels.

Double denim can work if done carefully: combining a lighter jacket with darker jeans or vice versa. Accessories like chains, caps, or sneakers tie the look together. Denim streetwear is perfect for casual days when you want a touch of rugged character.

Pro Tip: *Avoid perfectly matching denim shades. Instead, contrast light and dark tones or add in a bold piece (like a hoodie in a bright color) to break up the monotony.*

Trends

Inspiration

Textiles

Notes

Details

Swatches

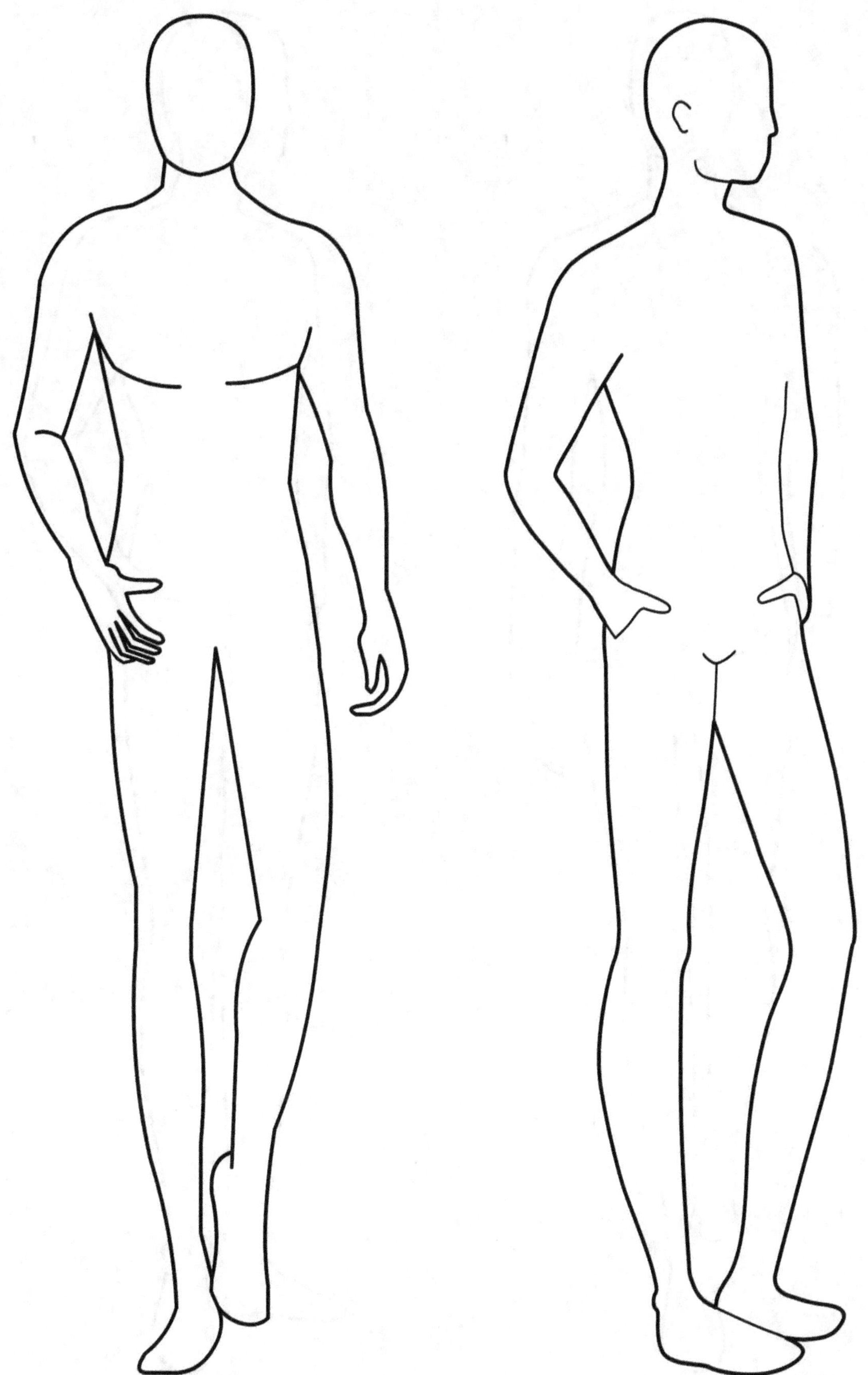

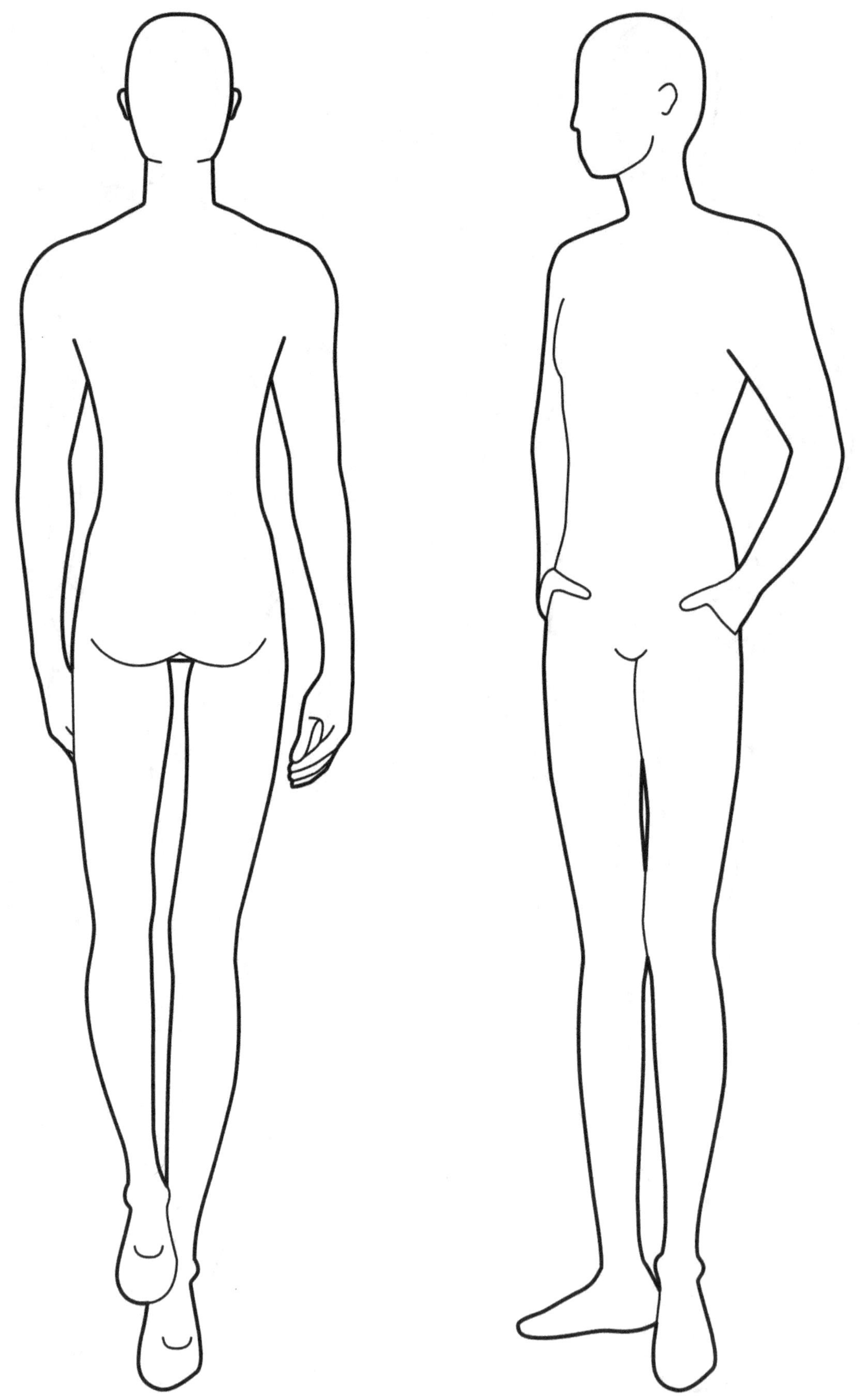

Your Notes & Inspiration Photos

This page is your personal mood board. Use it to document your style experiments, capture inspirations, and build a record of your design journey.

- Paste magazine cutouts, fabric samples, or outfit sketches.
- Write notes about what worked, what you'd like to improve, and how you imagine the design in real life.
- Keep track of recurring themes or shapes that define your aesthetic.

Pro Tip*: The strongest collections often come from small ideas. Save everything that catches your eye – it may become the seed of your next great design.*

Outfit Inspiration:
Office Chic and Runway Glam

Power Suiting + Sustainable Menswear Glam

Office Chic Inspiration

Power suiting relies on sharp tailoring and commanding presence. Structured blazers with broad shoulders, worn over fitted shirts and slim trousers, create authority. Dark shades like navy or black paired with polished shoes complete the ensemble. Accessories stay minimal but intentional.

Runway Glam Inspiration

Sustainable glam proves men's fashion can be responsible and stylish. Outfits crafted from recycled fabrics or natural fibers create runway-ready impact. Neutral tones, clean tailoring, and eco-conscious accessories showcase ethical luxury without compromise.

Fashion Practice Guide & Notes

Men's fashion is also about practicality. Clothes should balance style with comfort and functionality.

How to Use This Page:
- Sketch an outfit for a specific use (work, gym, weekend).
- Consider movement and comfort.
- Add notes about fabrics and practicality.

Reflection & Notes:

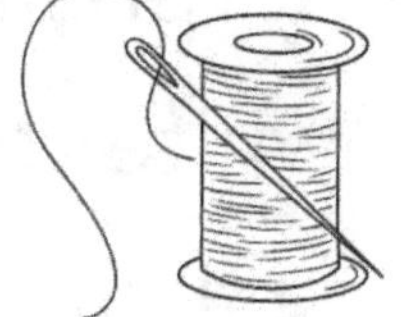

- Did I merge comfort with style?
- Which element adds most utility?
- How could I adapt this design?

Pro Tip: *Functionality gives men's fashion lasting appeal.*

____

____

____

____

____

____

____

____

____

Outfit Inspiration: Streetwear

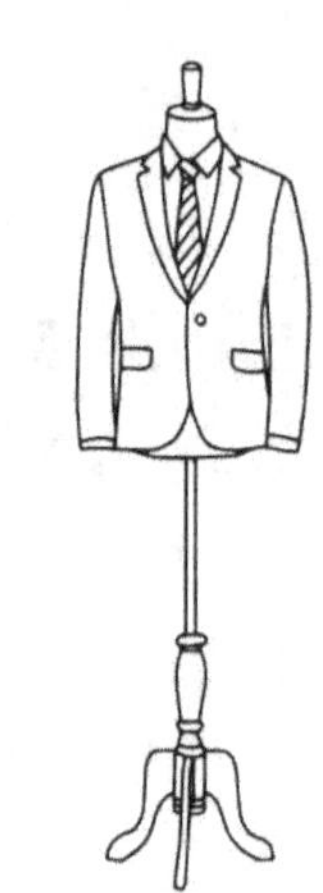

Monochrome Streetwear

The monochrome streetwear look is sleek, powerful, and surprisingly versatile. Dressing head-to-toe in black, white, or even earthy beige tones creates a unified and stylish vibe. The trick lies in mixing textures: matte cotton hoodies, glossy nylon jackets, and leather sneakers all add depth, even if the colors remain the same.

Monochrome outfits feel futuristic, intentional, and highly photogenic. They can be dressed up or down depending on accessories. All-black outfits, for example, always create a sharp street presence, while all-white has a fresh, minimalist energy.

Pro Tip: *Monochrome doesn't mean boring – use texture play (denim, nylon, wool, leather) to keep the outfit dynamic. Accessories like caps, belts, or layered chains add subtle contrast without breaking the theme.*

Trends

Inspiration

Textiles

Notes

Details

Swatches

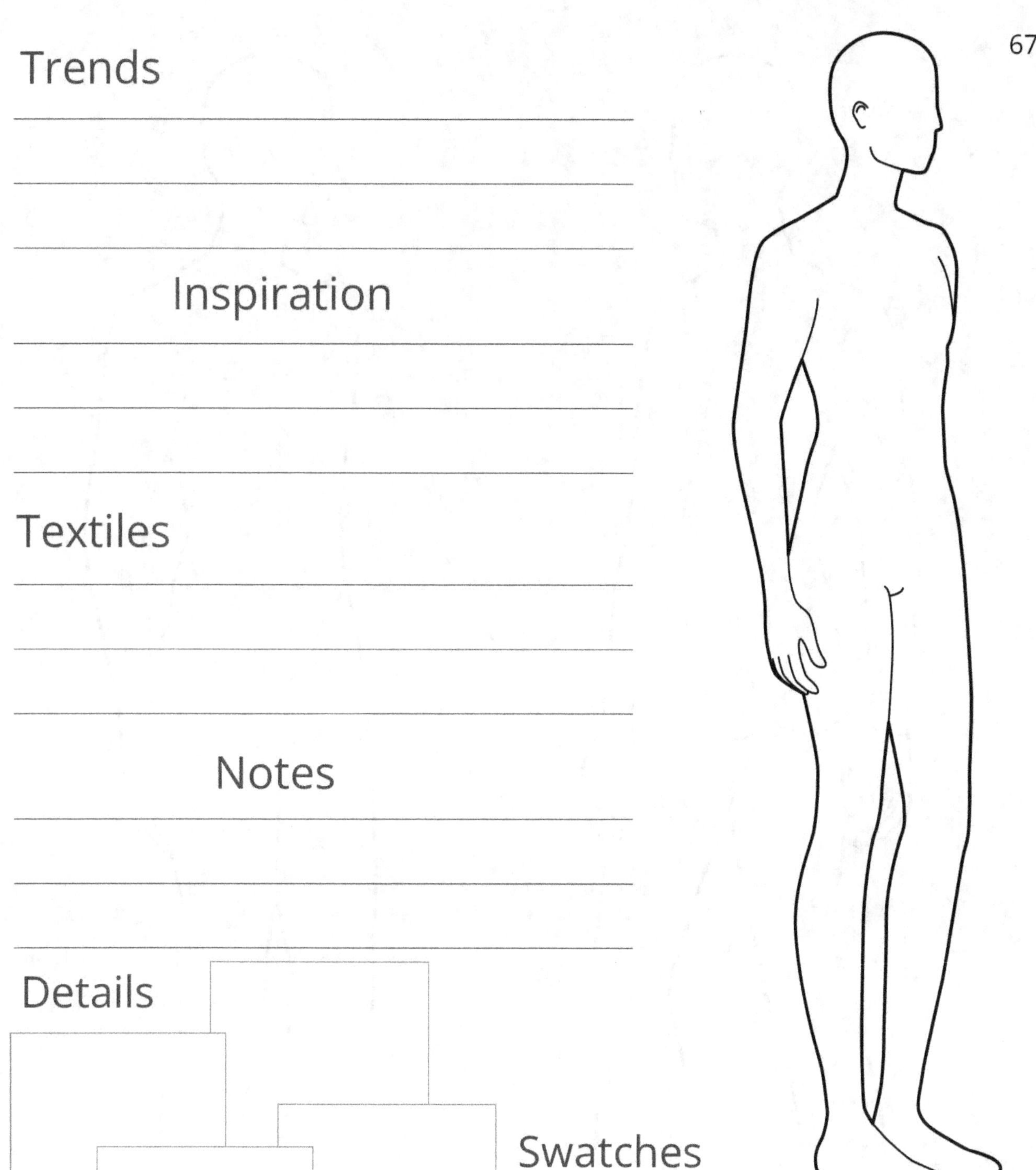

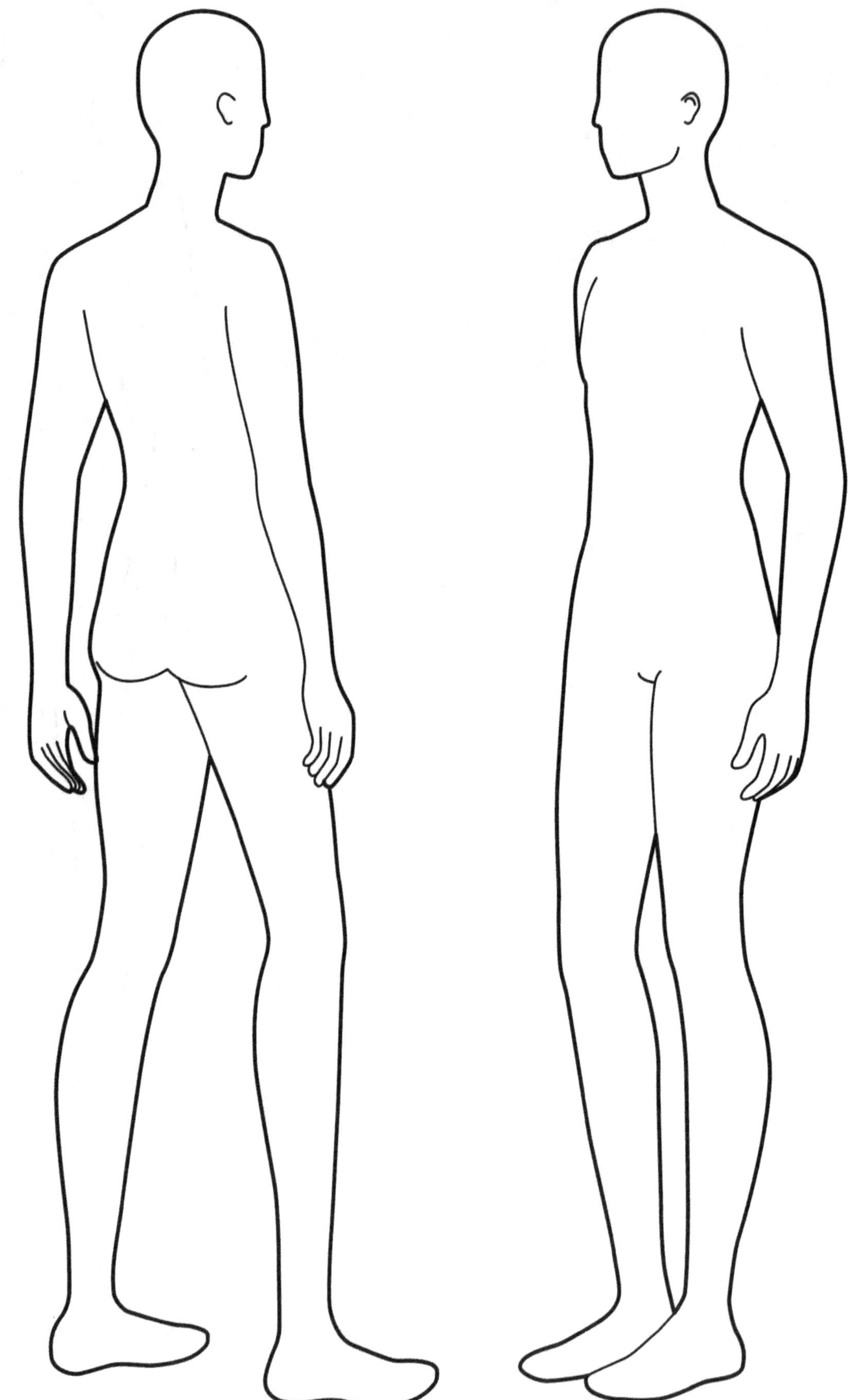

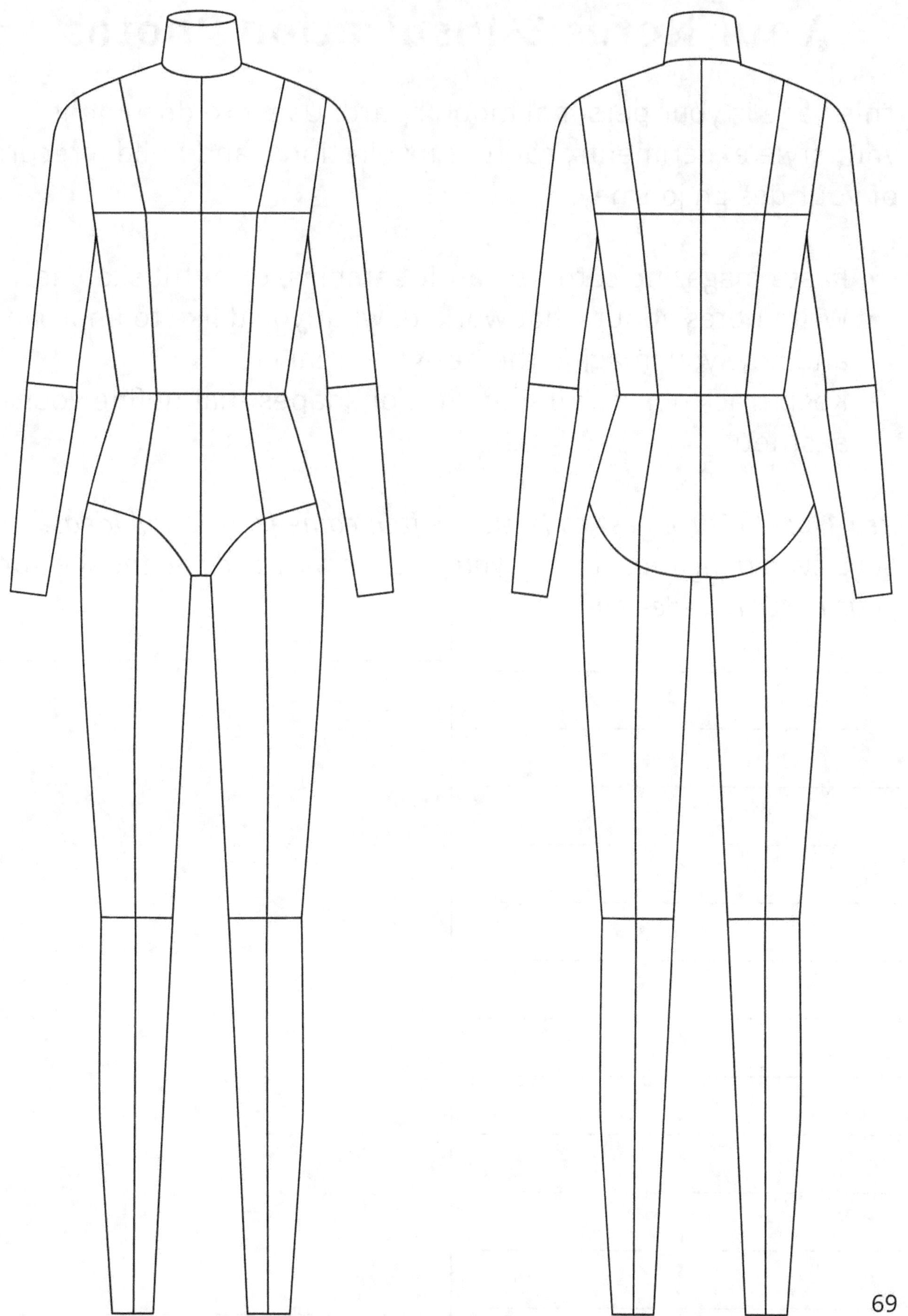

This page is your personal mood board. Use it to document your style experiments, capture inspirations, and build a record of your design journey.

- Paste magazine cutouts, fabric samples, or outfit sketches.
- Write notes about what worked, what you'd like to improve, and how you imagine the design in real life.
- Keep track of recurring themes or shapes that define your aesthetic.

Pro Tip: *The strongest collections often come from small ideas. Save everything that catches your eye – it may become the seed of your next great design.*

Outfit Inspiration:
Office Chic and Runway Glam

Casual Friday + Haute Couture Menswear

Office Chic Inspiration

Casual Fridays allow for relaxed refinement. Dark denim paired with a blazer and a crisp shirt strikes the right balance. Loafers or Chelsea boots elevate the look, while accessories like a leather belt or watch keep it professional. Comfort and polish coexist seamlessly here.

Runway Glam Inspiration

Haute couture menswear embodies craftsmanship and artistry. Hand-stitched embellishments, custom tailoring, and luxurious fabrics like silk or velvet create show-stopping ensembles. Jackets with exaggerated lapels or layered embroidery elevate everyday garments into art.

.

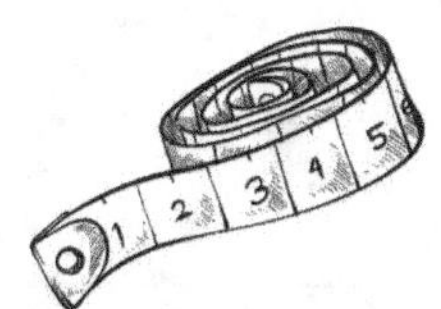

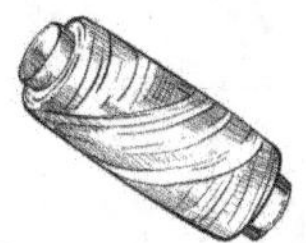

Fashion Practice Guide & Notes

Textures bring depth to men's outfits. Wool, denim, leather, or knits can completely shift the look.

How to Use This Page:
- Sketch a layered outfit and label fabrics.
- Mix heavy and light textures (wool coat with cotton tee).
- Write notes about how they interact.

Reflection & Notes:
- Which combo worked best?
- Did textures enhance the silhouette?
- How would I refine the sketch?

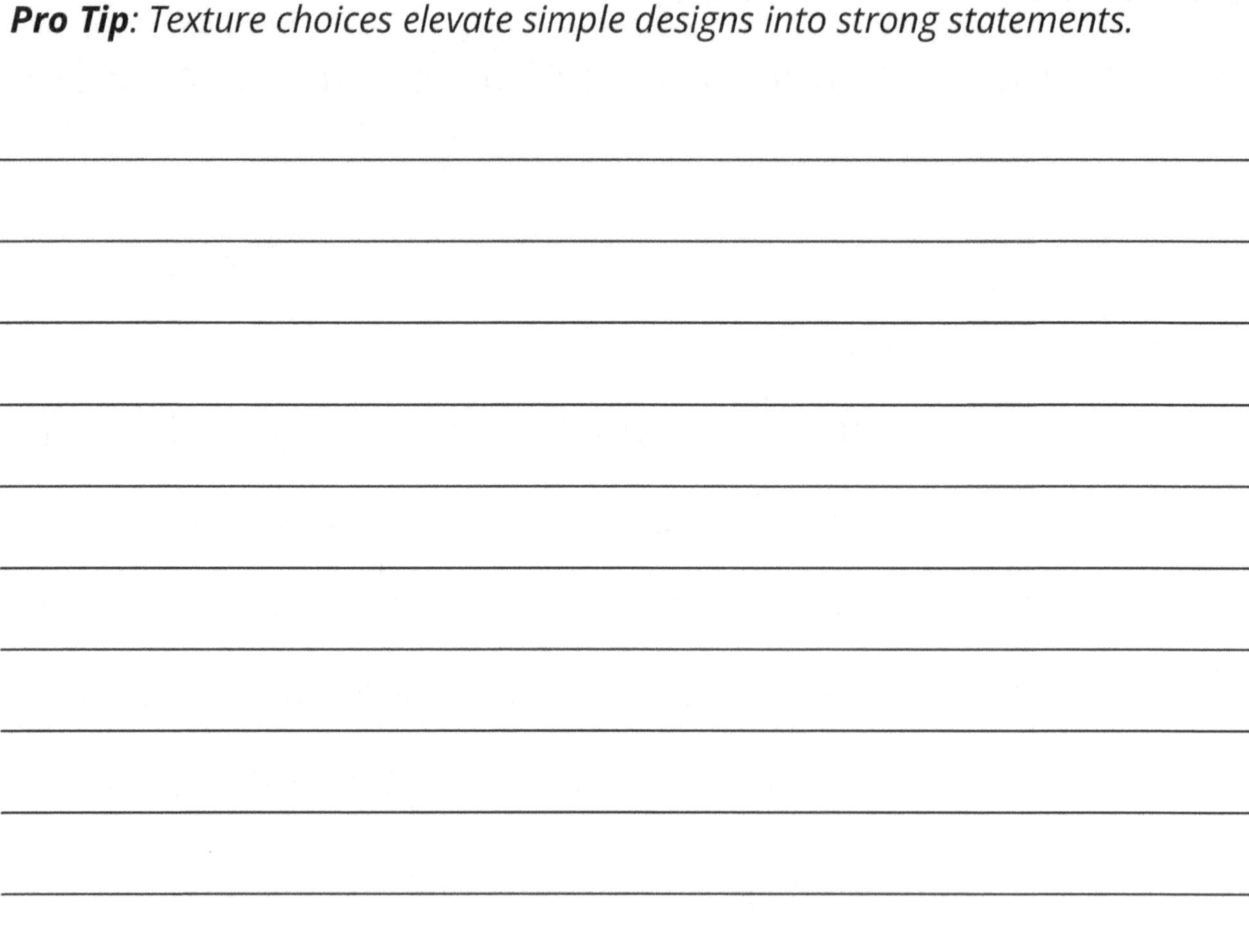

Pro Tip: Texture choices elevate simple designs into strong statements.

____

____

____

____

____

____

____

____

____

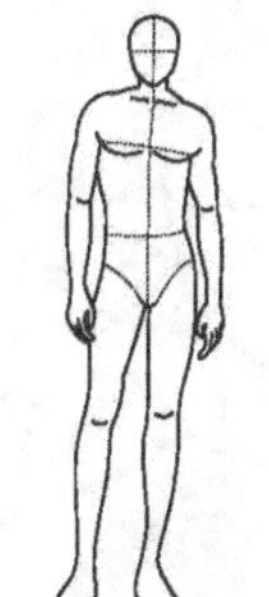

Outfit Inspiration: Streetwear

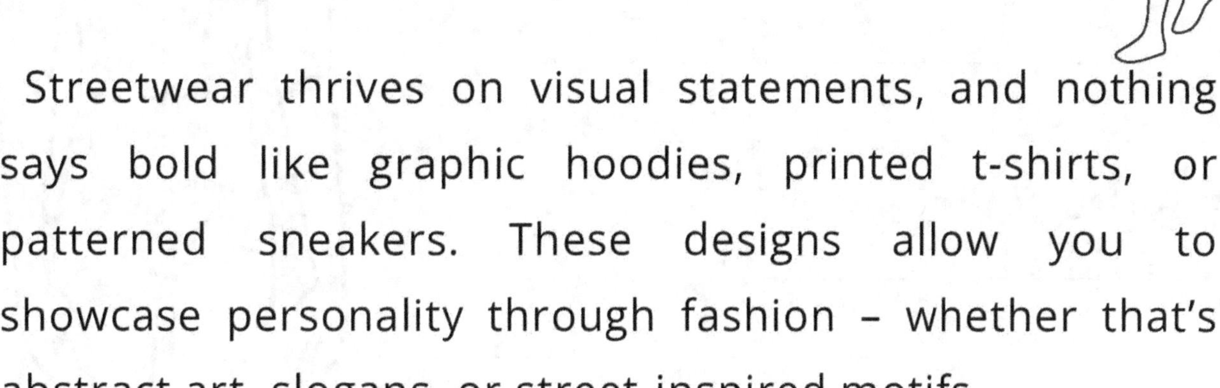

Graphic & Bold Prints

Streetwear thrives on visual statements, and nothing says bold like graphic hoodies, printed t-shirts, or patterned sneakers. These designs allow you to showcase personality through fashion – whether that's abstract art, slogans, or street-inspired motifs.

Pair bold prints with neutral basics to avoid overwhelming the look. For example, a hoodie covered in colorful graphics can be balanced with black joggers and plain sneakers. The key is to let one item shine while keeping the rest of the outfit simple.

Pro Tip: One statement piece is enough. If you wear a loud hoodie, keep the pants and shoes neutral. Otherwise, the look can feel cluttered rather than expressive.

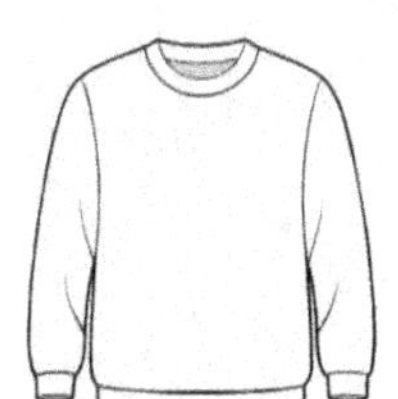

Trends

Inspiration

Textiles

Notes

Details

Swatches

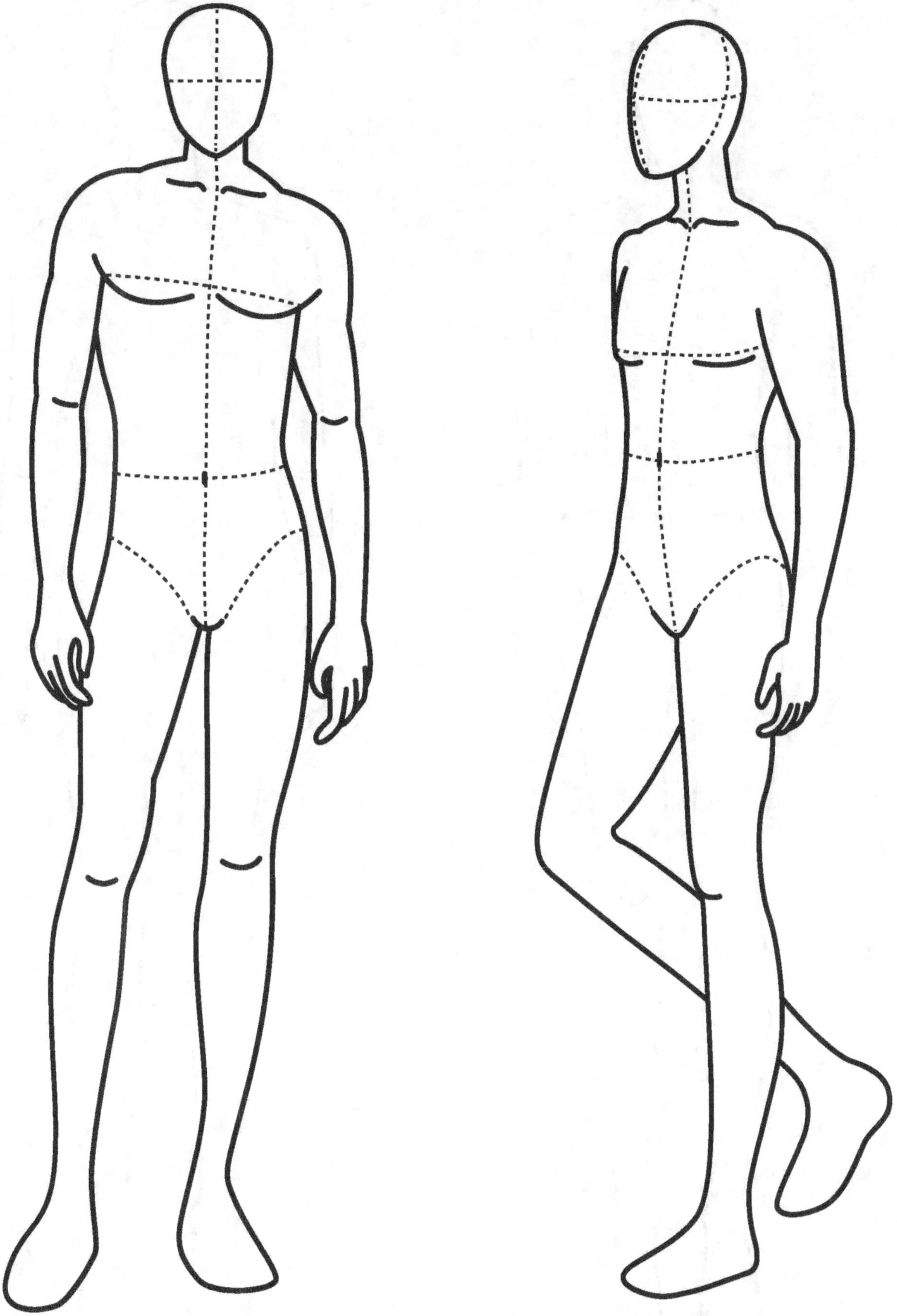

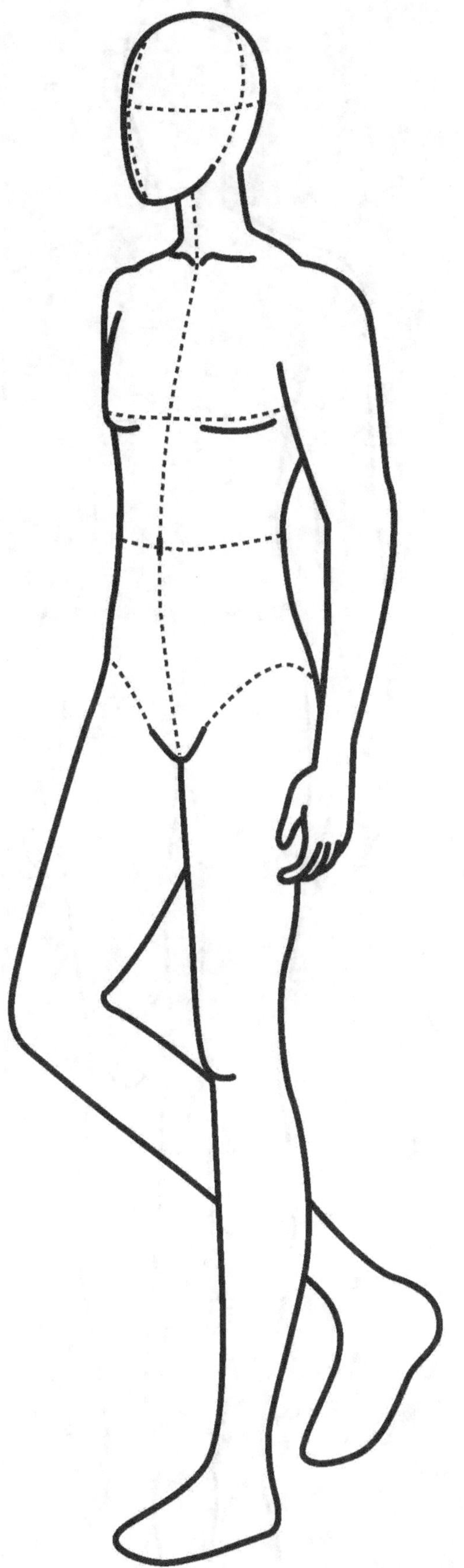

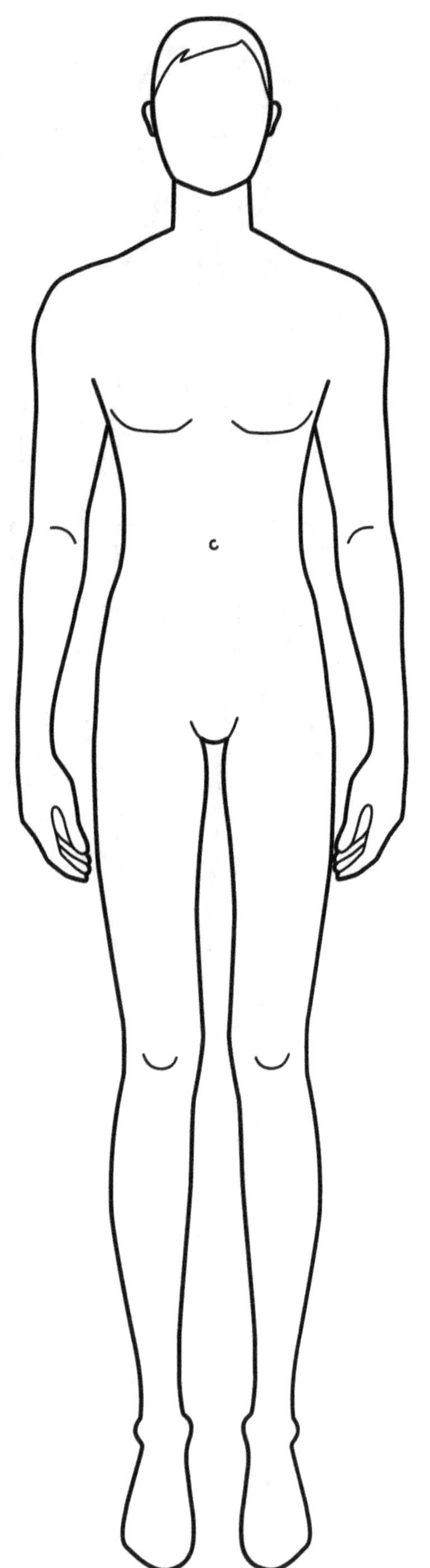
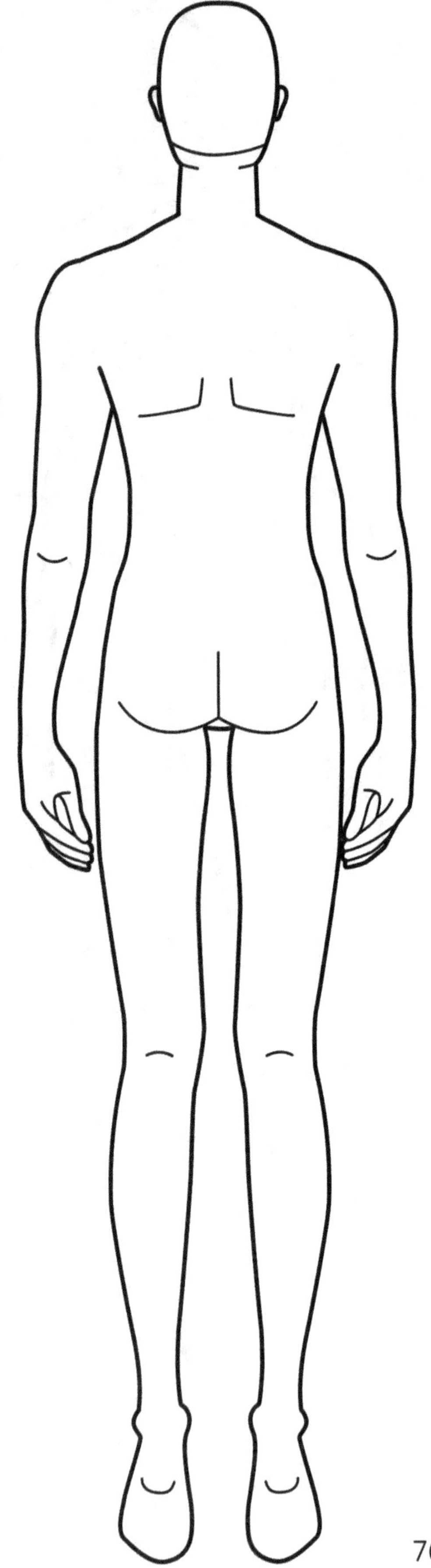

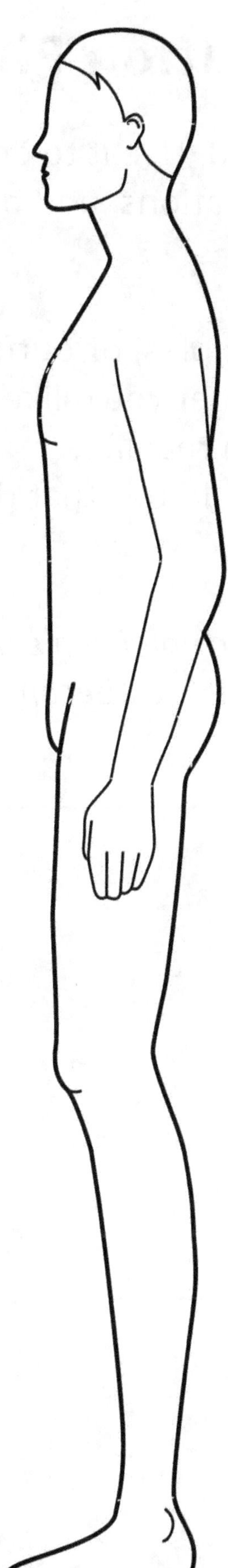 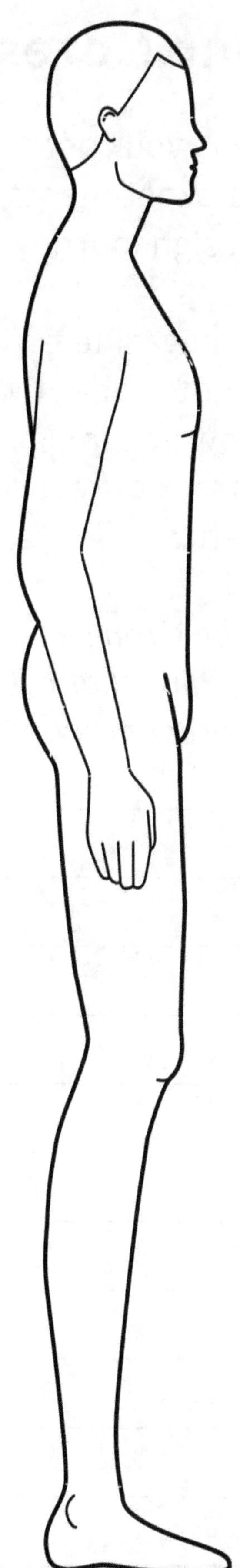

Your Notes & Inspiration Photos

This page is your personal mood board. Use it to document your style experiments, capture inspirations, and build a record of your design journey.

- Paste magazine cutouts, fabric samples, or outfit sketches.
- Write notes about what worked, what you'd like to improve, and how you imagine the design in real life.
- Keep track of recurring themes or shapes that define your aesthetic.

Pro Tip: The strongest collections often come from small ideas. Save everything that catches your eye – it may become the seed of your next great design.

Outfit Inspiration:
Office Chic and Runway Glam

Monochrome Office Style + Minimal Glam

Office Chic Inspiration

A monochrome palette creates instant cohesion. An all-black, all-grey, or all-navy outfit built with varied textures makes a bold yet professional impression. A wool blazer, cotton shirt, and leather belt in the same tone showcase refinement through simplicity.

Runway Glam Inspiration

Minimal glam for men is sleek and powerful. Tailored suits or streamlined coats in bold solid colors emphasize structure. A single standout accessory – perhaps a metallic belt or statement shoes – adds just enough drama. The beauty lies in restraint and sharp cuts.

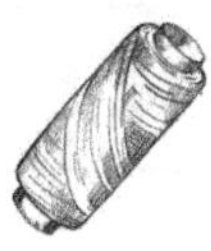 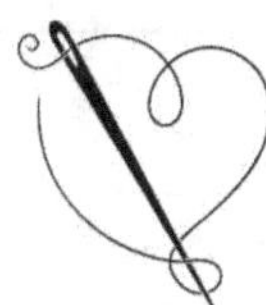 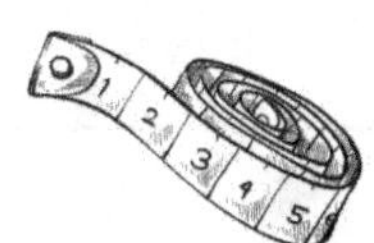

Fashion Practice Guide & Notes

Accessories define men's style more than people realize. Use this page to see how they shift an outfit's mood.

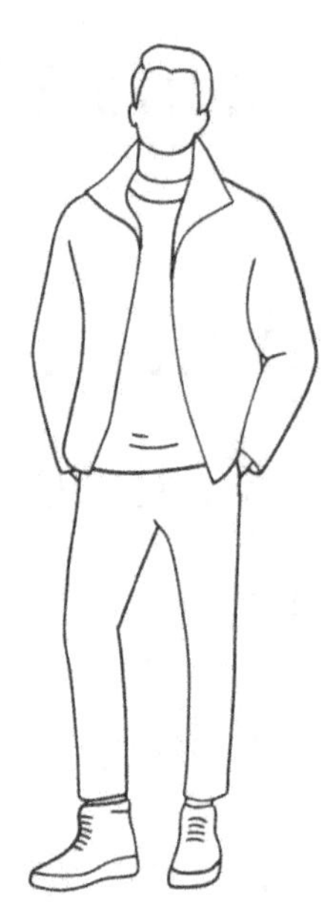

How to Use This Page:
- Start with a base look (shirt + trousers).
- Add 2–3 different accessories (watch, bag, hat, shoes).
- Write which version feels strongest.

Reflection & Notes:
- Which accessory added most character?
- Did it overpower or enhance the outfit?
- How could I refine the balance?

Pro Tip: *A single accessory can turn casual into iconic.*

____

____

____

____

____

____

____

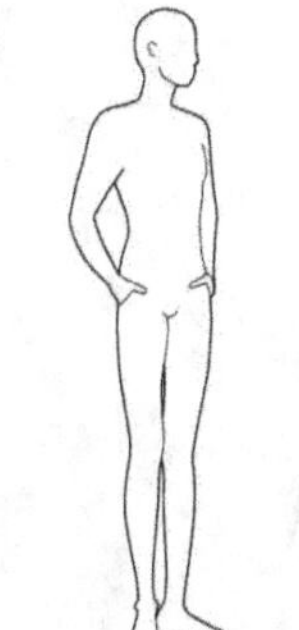

Outfit Inspiration: Streetwear

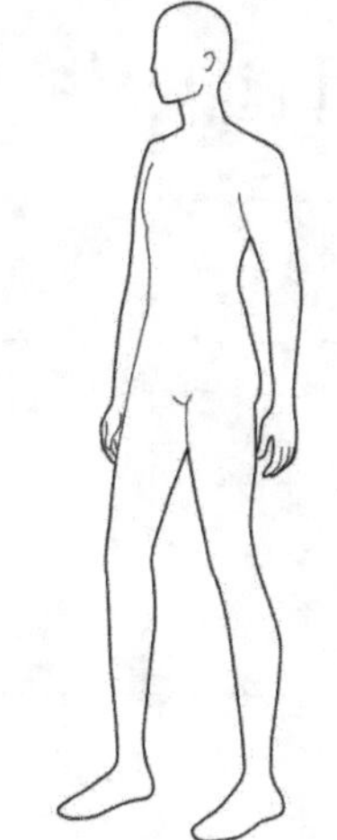

Military-Inspired Streetwear

Cargo pants, camo prints, utility jackets, and combat boots bring a rugged, tactical vibe to the streetwear world. This style is rooted in practicality: big pockets, sturdy fabrics, and earthy colors like olive, khaki, and black. But functionality doesn't mean boring. Military-inspired streetwear is adaptable – combine a camo jacket with slim joggers, or wear cargo pants with a simple hoodie. The outcome feels grounded and strong.

This style resonates with those who want a blend of toughness and modern street edge.

Pro Tip*: Stick to an earthy color palette – olive green, khaki, beige, and black work best. Add one modern twist (like sleek sneakers) to keep the look street-ready instead of costume-like.*

Trends

Inspiration

Textiles

Notes

Details

Swatches

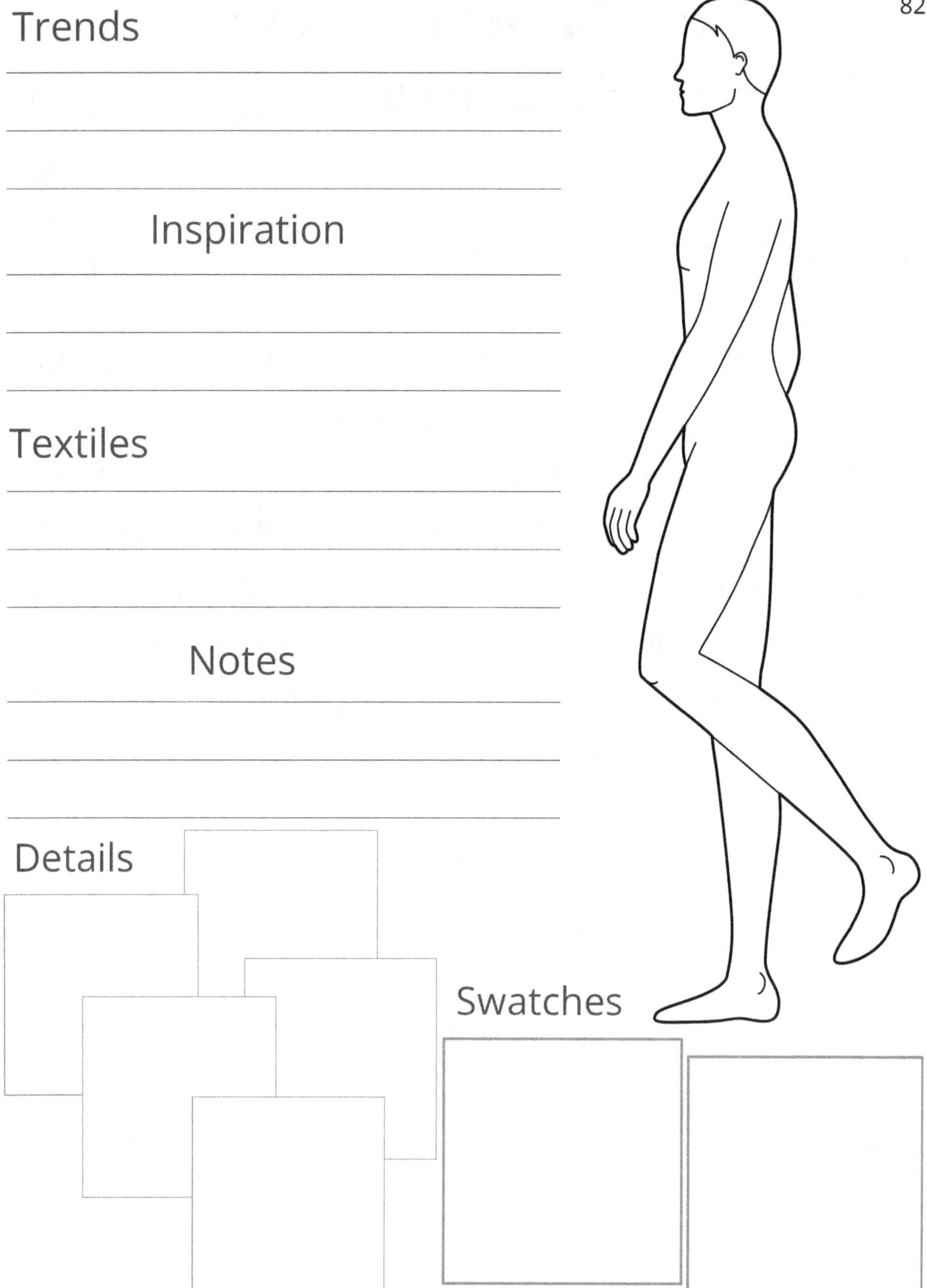

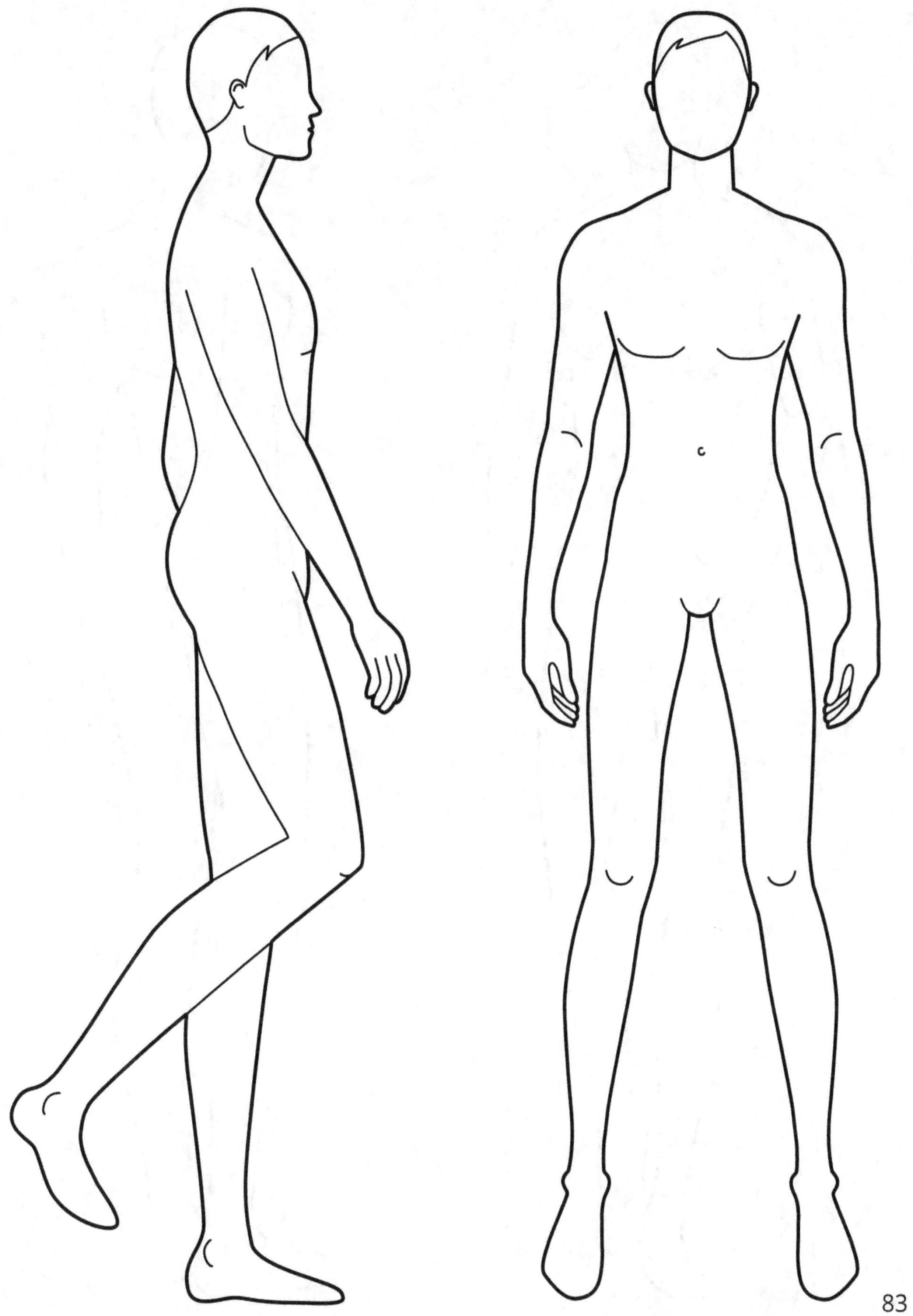

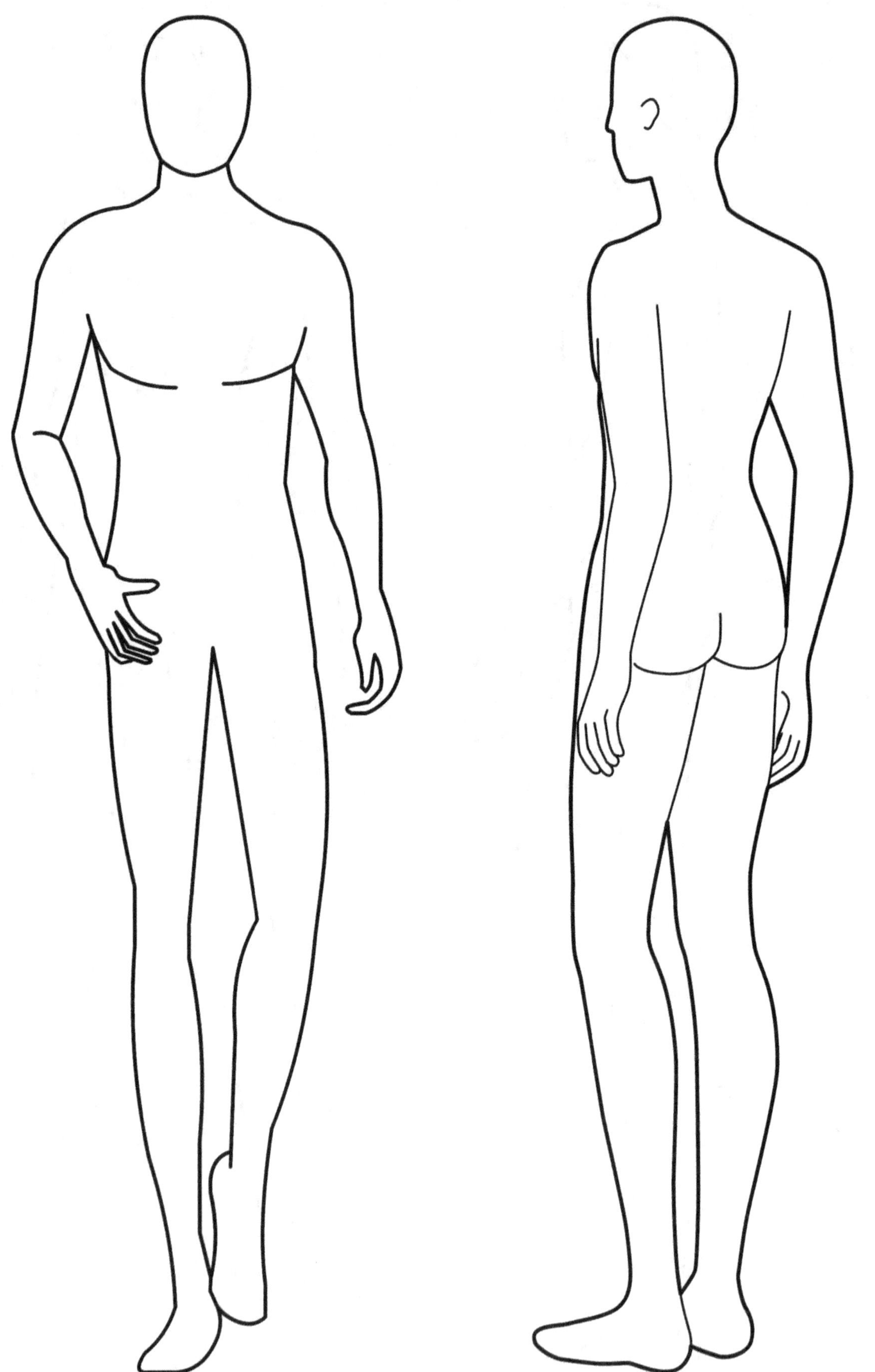

Your Notes & Inspiration Photos

This page is your personal mood board. Use it to document your style experiments, capture inspirations, and build a record of your design journey.

- Paste magazine cutouts, fabric samples, or outfit sketches.
- Write notes about what worked, what you'd like to improve, and how you imagine the design in real life.
- Keep track of recurring themes or shapes that define your aesthetic.

Pro Tip: *The strongest collections often come from small ideas. Save everything that catches your eye – it may become the seed of your next great design.*

Outfit Inspiration:
Office Chic and Runway Glam

Smart-Casual Hybrid + Futuristic Elegance

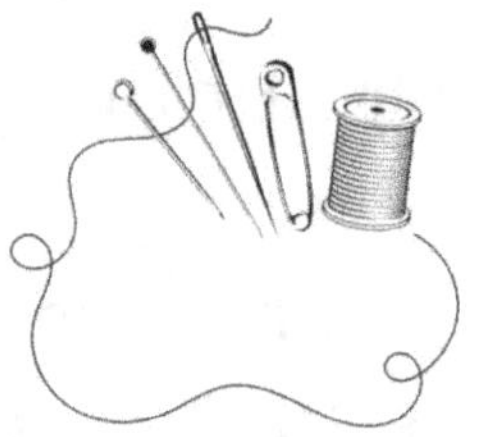

Office Chic Inspiration

Smart-casual looks blend professionalism with ease. Pair chinos with a button-down shirt, layering with a cardigan or unstructured blazer. Leather sneakers or loafers complete the ensemble. This look fits modern workplaces that value adaptability and personal style.

Runway Glam Inspiration

Futuristic elegance blends innovation with sophistication. Tailored jackets in metallic or iridescent fabrics, slim trousers, and subtle geometric detailing create an elegant yet avant-garde aesthetic. Accessories remain minimal to let the structure and fabric shine.

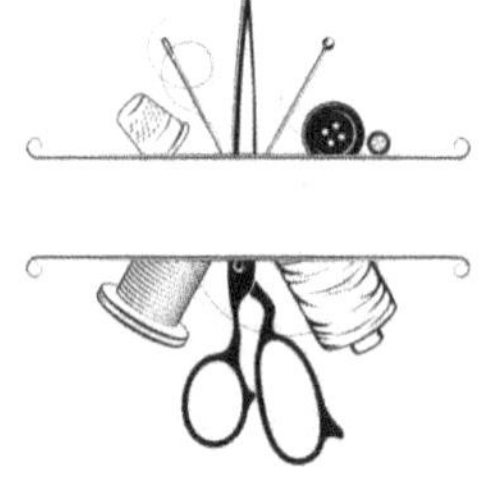

Fashion Practice Guide & Notes

Proportion is key in men's tailoring. Use this page to practice balance between shoulders, waist, and leg length.

How to Use This Page:
- Focus on jackets, trousers, and body ratios.
- Try fitted vs. relaxed cuts.
- Write notes on what looked most natural.

Reflection & Notes:
- Which proportion worked best?
- Did the outfit look balanced?
- What will I adjust in future sketches?

Pro Tip: *Strong proportions make designs timeless.*

Outfit Inspiration: Streetwear

Skate Culture Style

Skateboarding has influenced streetwear for decades, giving rise to oversized tees, baggy jeans, and practical sneakers like skate shoes. Flannels tied around the waist or worn loosely over t-shirts add another layer of casual cool. This style embodies rebellion, independence, and creativity.

What makes skate streetwear iconic is its raw authenticity – clothes are worn for movement and function, but they also carry cultural weight. It's as much about lifestyle as it is about appearance.

Pro Tip: *Keep accessories minimal – a cap, wristband, or backpack is enough. The laid-back vibe works best when it feels unplanned and effortless.*

Trends

Inspiration

Textiles

Notes

Details

Swatches

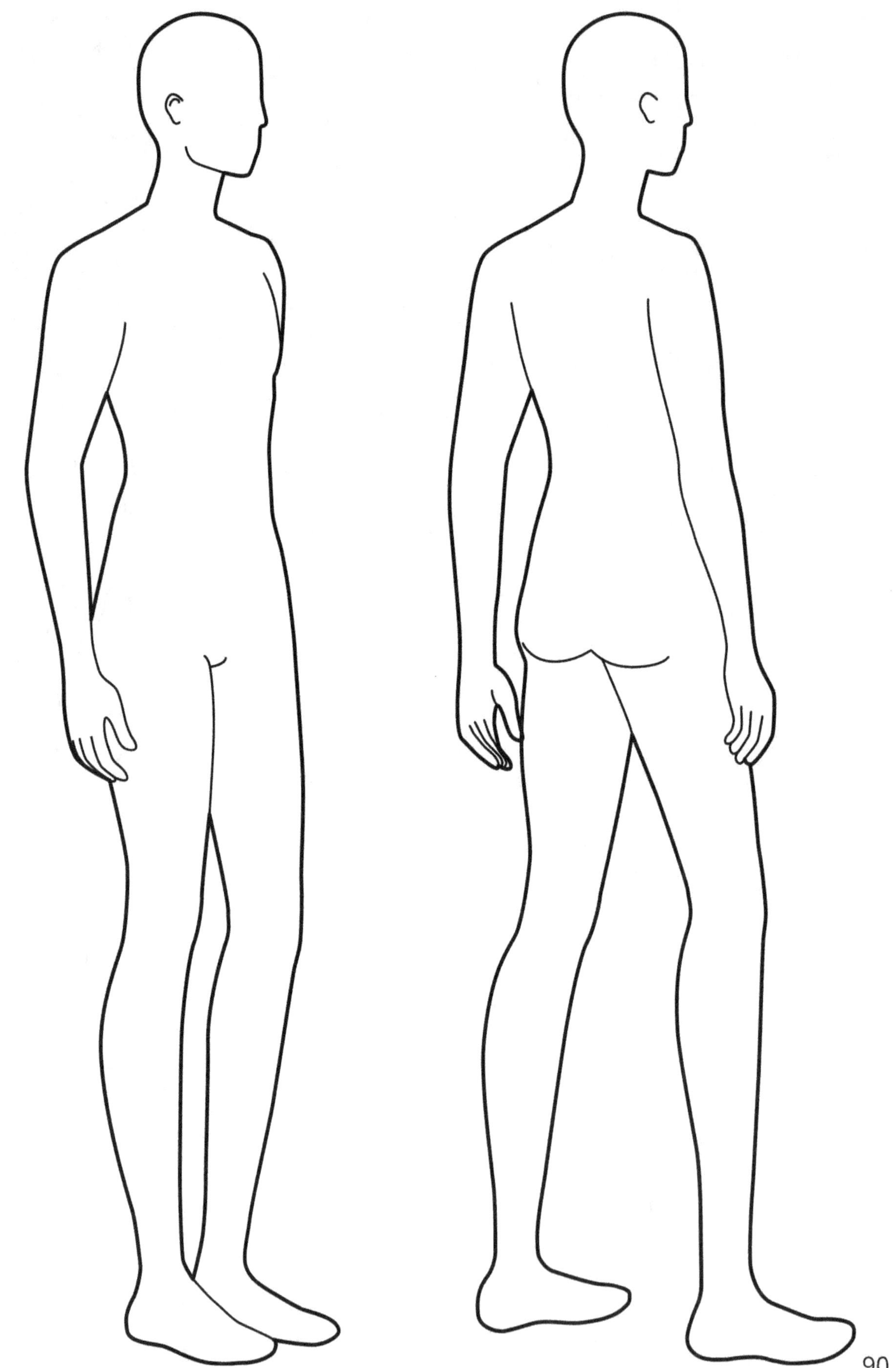

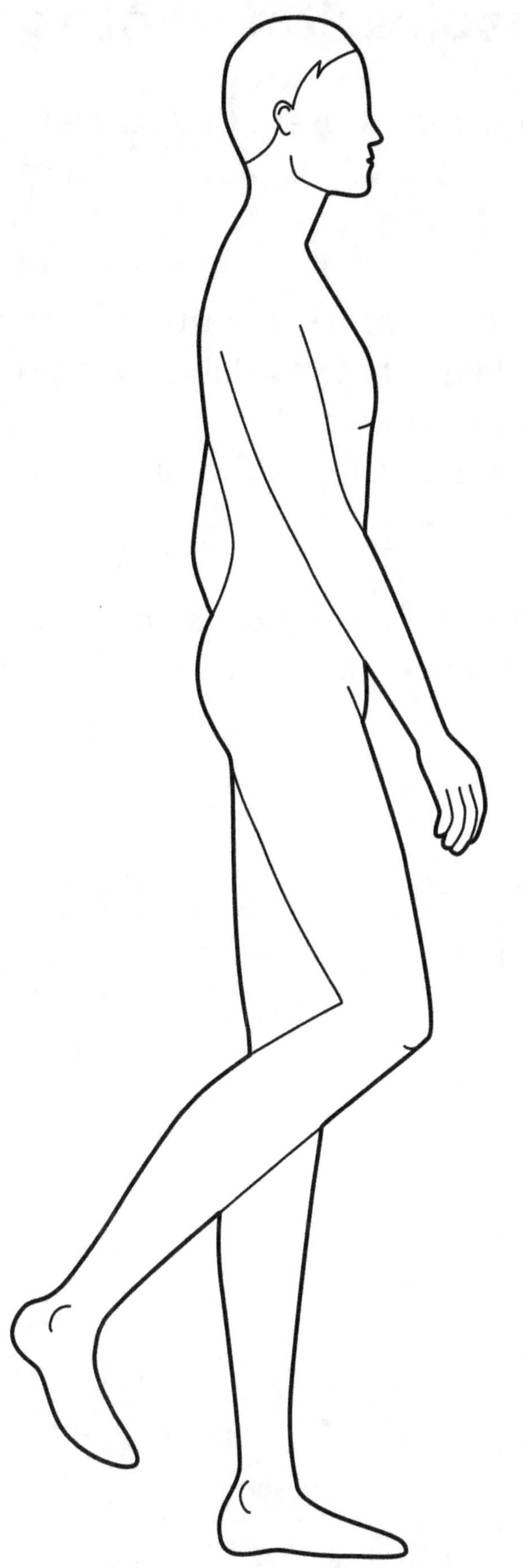
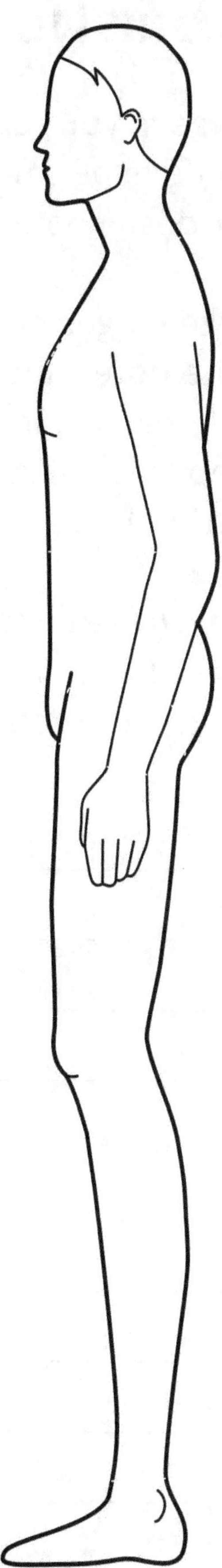

Your Notes & Inspiration Photos

This page is your personal mood board. Use it to document your style experiments, capture inspirations, and build a record of your design journey.

- Paste magazine cutouts, fabric samples, or outfit sketches.
- Write notes about what worked, what you'd like to improve, and how you imagine the design in real life.
- Keep track of recurring themes or shapes that define your aesthetic.

Pro Tip*: The strongest collections often come from small ideas. Save everything that catches your eye – it may become the seed of your next great design.*

Outfit Inspiration: Office Chic and Runway Glam

Modern Layering + Festival Spark

Office Chic Inspiration

Layering adds versatility and character. A vest under a blazer, a turtleneck beneath a shirt, or lightweight outerwear over a dress shirt brings depth. Choosing complementary textures, like wool and cotton, elevates the style.

Runway Glam Inspiration

Festival glam for men thrives on sparkle and boldness. Sequined blazers, embroidered jackets, or metallic trousers exude energy. Playful layering and vibrant color palettes capture the celebratory mood, while accessories like statement hats or embellished belts enhance individuality.

Fashion Practice Guide & Notes

Colors set the tone of men's outfits-muted neutrals vs. bold statements. Use this page to test palettes.

How to Use This Page:
- Sketch one base outfit.
- Apply 2–3 color schemes (earthy, monochrome, bright).
- Note how mood shifts with each.

Reflection & Notes:
- Which palette fit the concept best?
- Did colors harmonize or clash?
- How would I use it again?

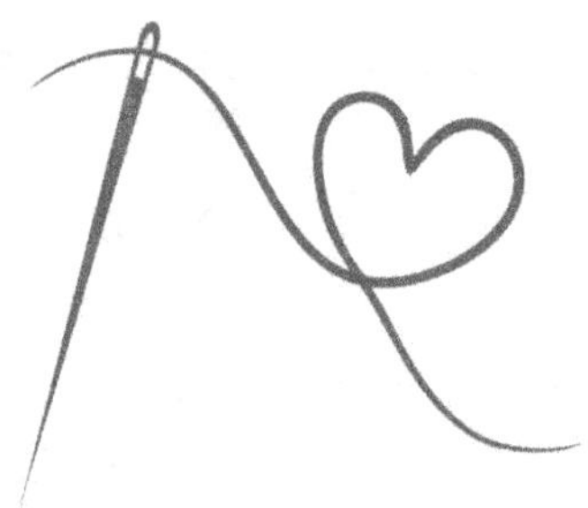

Pro Tip: Color is the silent language of style.

Outfit Inspiration: Streetwear

Techwear Streetwear

Techwear is futuristic, functional, and fashion-forward. Think waterproof fabrics, adjustable straps, hidden zippers, and layered pockets. Outfits often appear tactical but are designed with a sleek, modern silhouette. Black and grey dominate the palette, with occasional neon accents for emphasis.

This style makes a strong statement and is perfect for those who see fashion as performance gear. It's not about blending in – it's about standing out while looking prepared for anything.

Pro Tip: *Start with a black base (cargo pants + utility jacket) and add one functional detail (a crossbody bag or neon strap). This makes the outfit wearable without going overboard.*

Trends

Inspiration

Textiles

Notes

Details

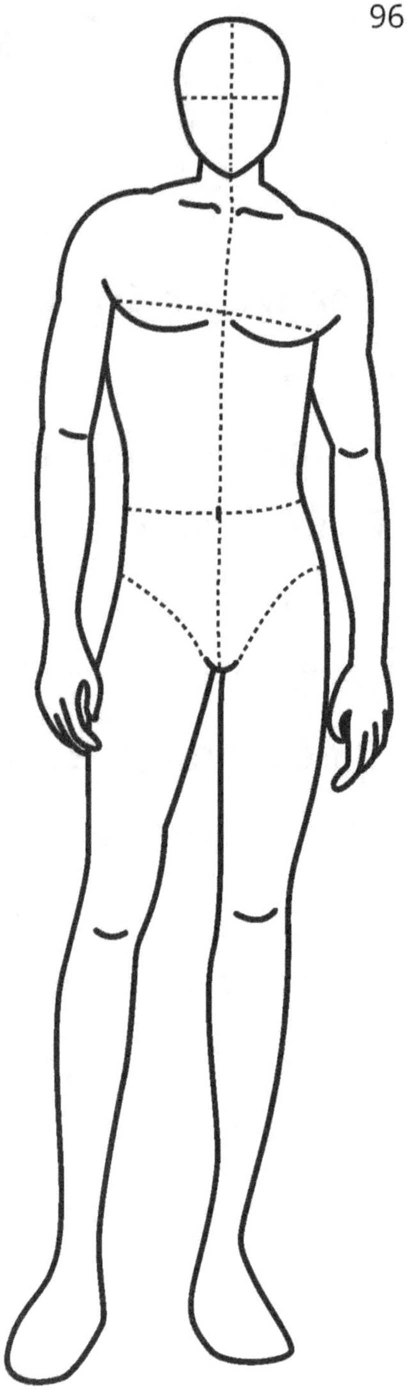

Swatches

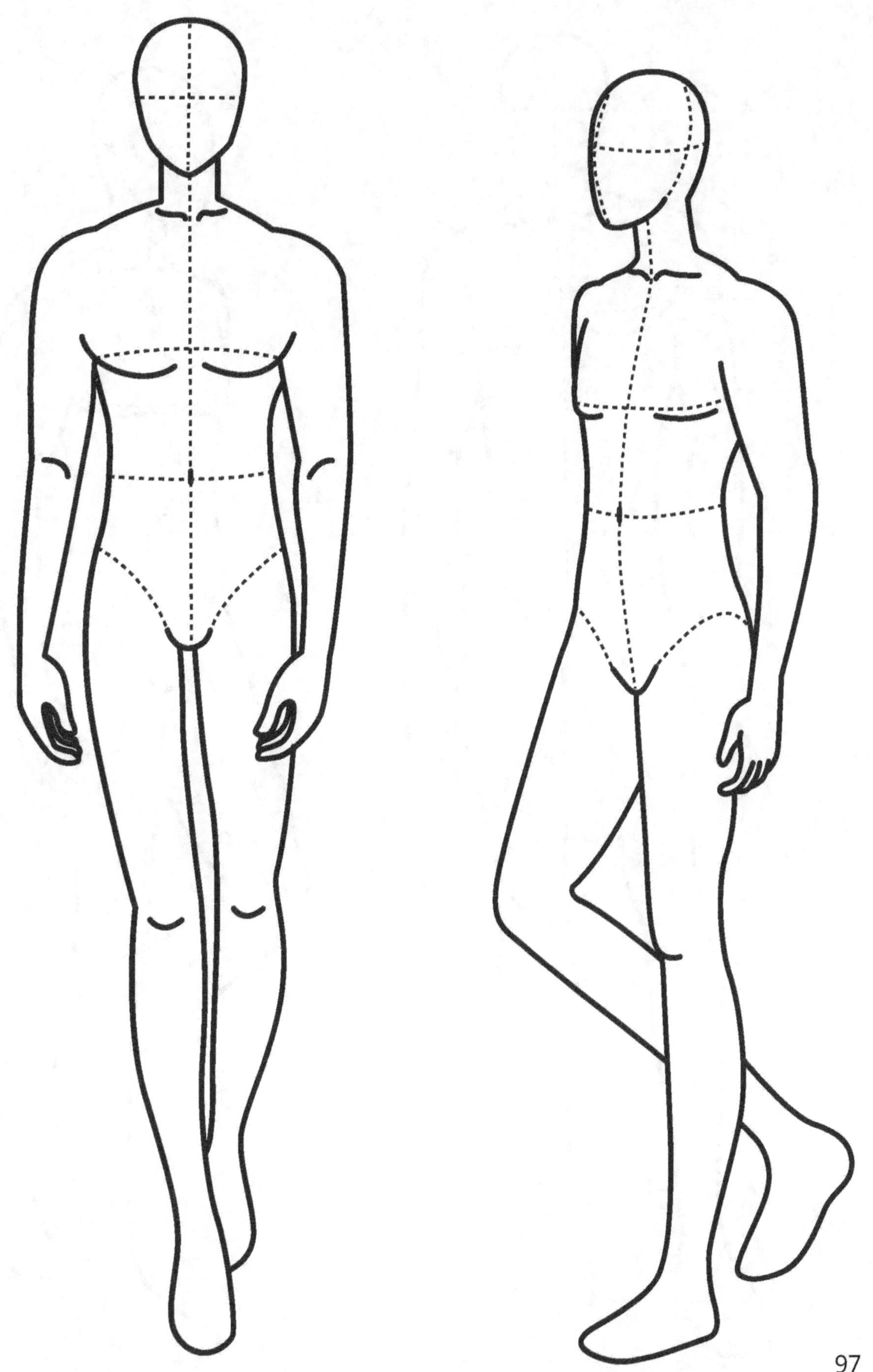

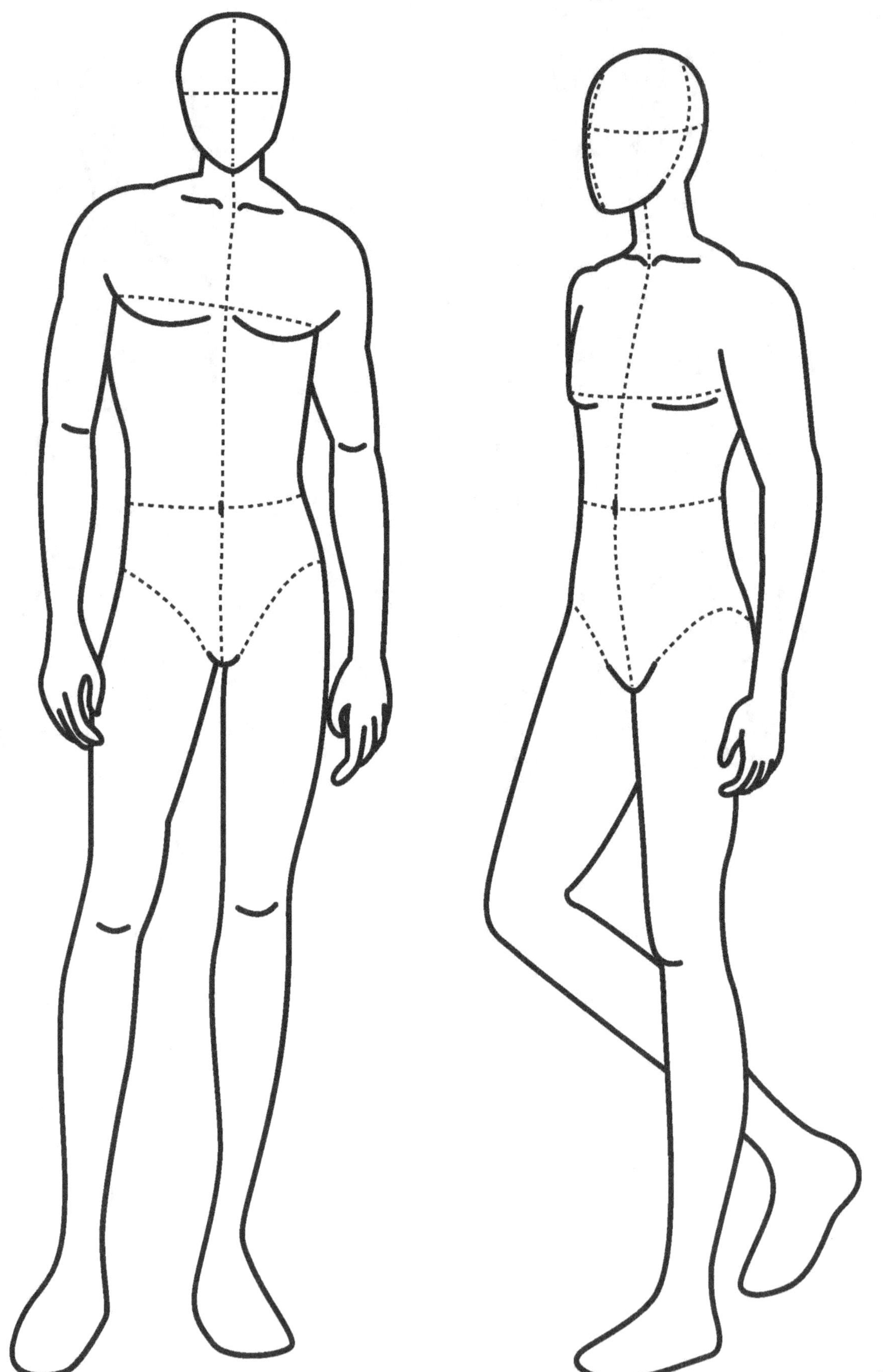

Your Notes & Inspiration Photos

This page is your personal mood board. Use it to document your style experiments, capture inspirations, and build a record of your design journey.

- Paste magazine cutouts, fabric samples, or outfit sketches.
- Write notes about what worked, what you'd like to improve, and how you imagine the design in real life.
- Keep track of recurring themes or shapes that define your aesthetic.

Pro Tip: *The strongest collections often come from small ideas. Save everything that catches your eye – it may become the seed of your next great design.*

Outfit Inspiration: Office Chic and Runway Glam

Elegant Office Uniform + Sustainable Couture

Office Chic Inspiration

Some workplaces lean on a uniform approach: tailored trousers, a neutral shirt, and a structured blazer. When elevated with quality fabrics and precise tailoring, this simplicity becomes elegance. Subtle accessories, such as slim ties or leather shoes, maintain a refined balance.

Runway Glam Inspiration

Sustainable couture emphasizes craftsmanship with eco-awareness. Recycled fabrics, natural dyes, and minimal-waste designs highlight both innovation and care for the planet. Full-length tailored coats or layered ensembles communicate responsibility and style.

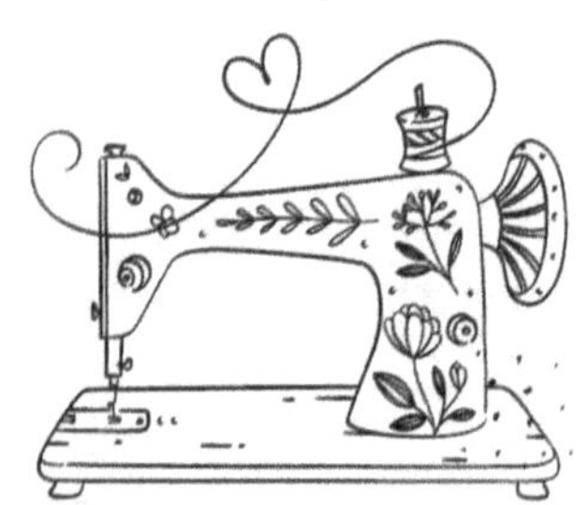

Fashion Practice Guide & Notes

Think in collections, not just single outfits. Men's fashion gains strength when pieces belong together.

How to Use This Page:
- Create 2–3 variations of the same theme.
- Keep a unifying detail (color, texture, silhouette).
- Note how they connect as a set.

Reflection & Notes:
- Did the pieces look cohesive?
- Which one stood out?
- How could I improve harmony?

Pro Tip: Consistency builds strong men's collections.

Outfit Inspiration: Streetwear

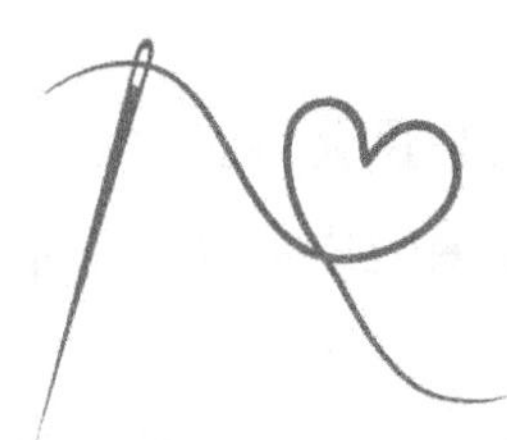

Minimalist Streetwear

Minimalist streetwear strips fashion back to the essentials. Clean lines, neutral colors, and no logos define this look. Think slim joggers, plain hoodies, and fresh sneakers. The focus is on fit and fabric quality, not flashy designs.

This style works in almost any situation – from casual days to semi-professional settings – because it avoids excess while maintaining urban character.

Pro Tip: *Invest in premium basics. A well-cut hoodie or high-quality sneakers can elevate even the simplest outfit into something refined.*

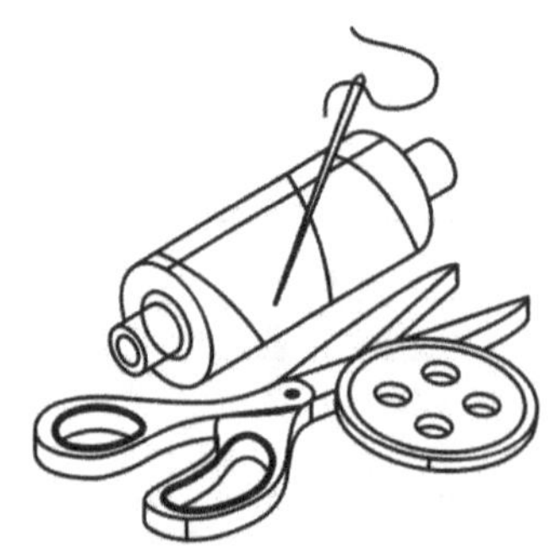

Trends

Inspiration

Textiles

Notes

Details

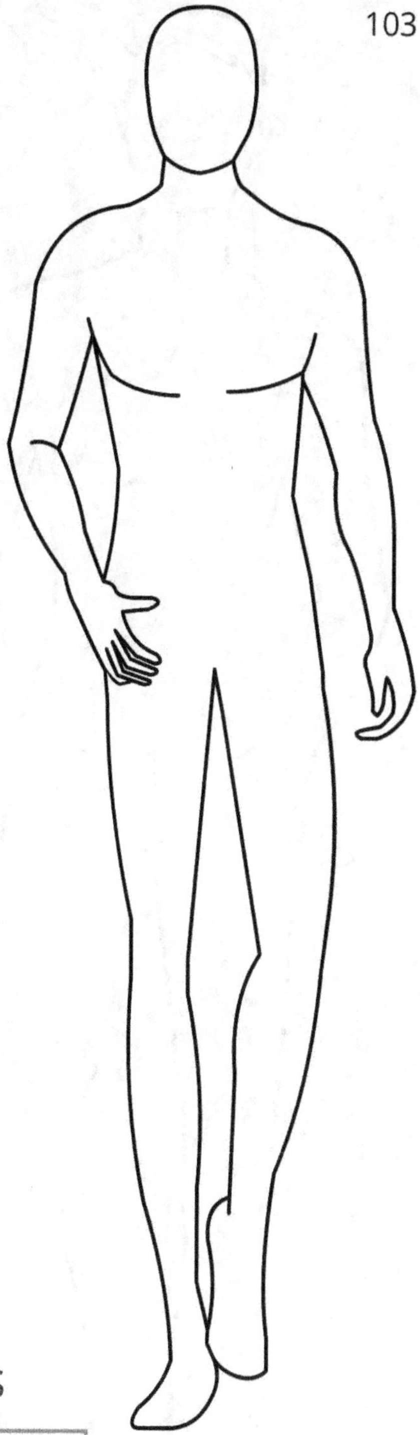

Swatches

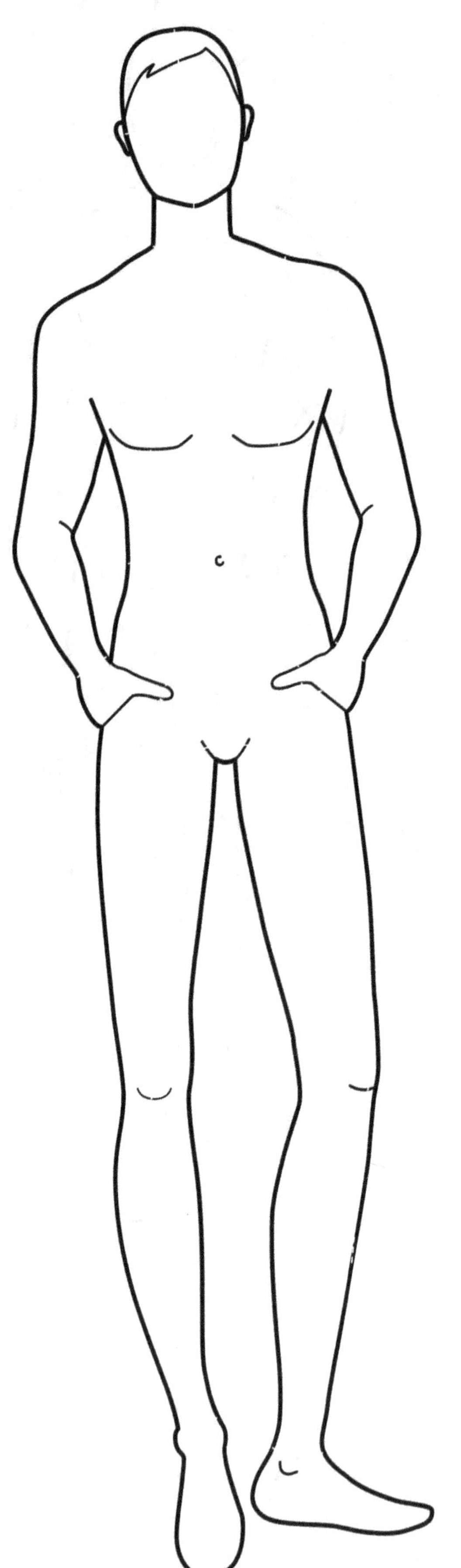
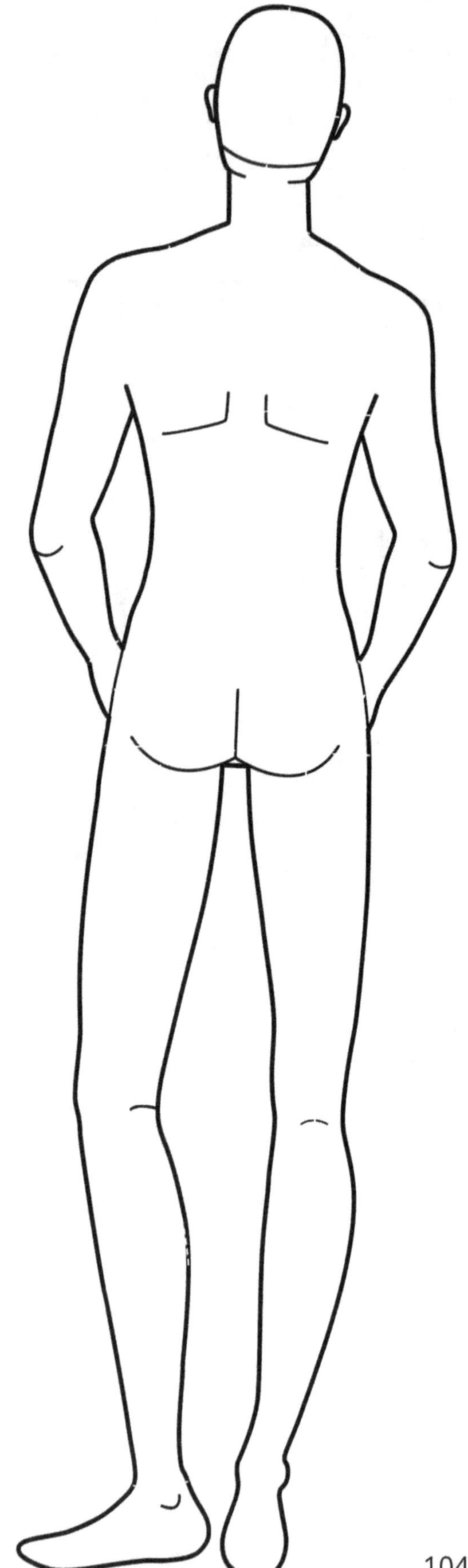

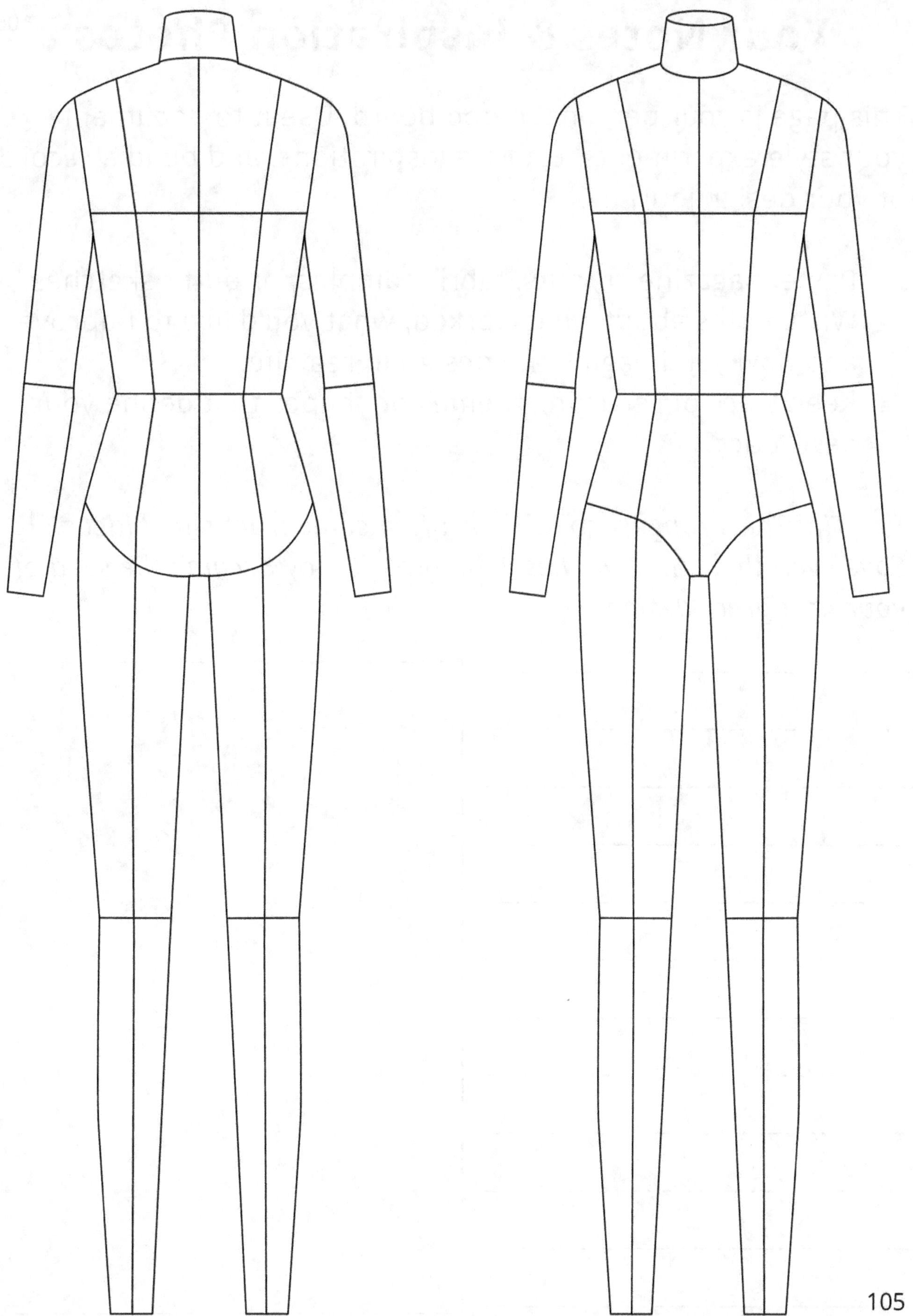

Your Notes & Inspiration Photos

This page is your personal mood board. Use it to document your style experiments, capture inspirations, and build a record of your design journey.

- Paste magazine cutouts, fabric samples, or outfit sketches.
- Write notes about what worked, what you'd like to improve, and how you imagine the design in real life.
- Keep track of recurring themes or shapes that define your aesthetic.

Pro Tip*: The strongest collections often come from small ideas. Save everything that catches your eye – it may become the seed of your next great design.*

Outfit Inspiration: Office Chic and Runway Glam

Trend-Adaptive Professional + Futuristic Showpiece

Office Chic Inspiration

Men can adapt subtle trends without losing professionalism. Cropped trousers paired with loafers, or muted pastels layered with neutrals, keep outfits fresh. Accessories like slim backpacks or modern glasses add functional elegance.

Runway Glam Inspiration

Futuristic showpieces demand attention. Sculptural jackets, illuminated details, or reflective fabrics redefine modern menswear. Footwear may include exaggerated soles or metallic finishes. These ensembles blur the line between art and clothing.

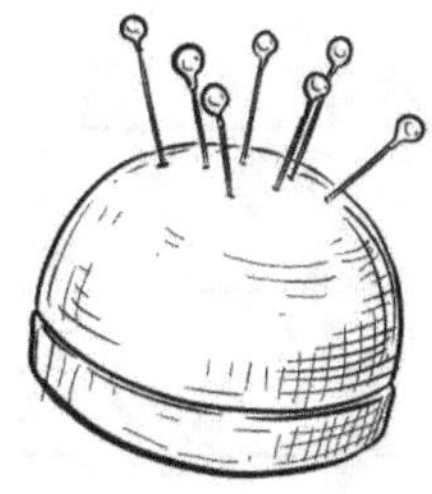

Fashion Practice Guide & Notes

Minimalism is powerful in men's fashion. Clean lines and subtle detail often speak louder than excess.

How to Use This Page:
- Design with max. 3 elements.
- Focus on silhouette and fit.
- Write how simplicity changed the vibe.

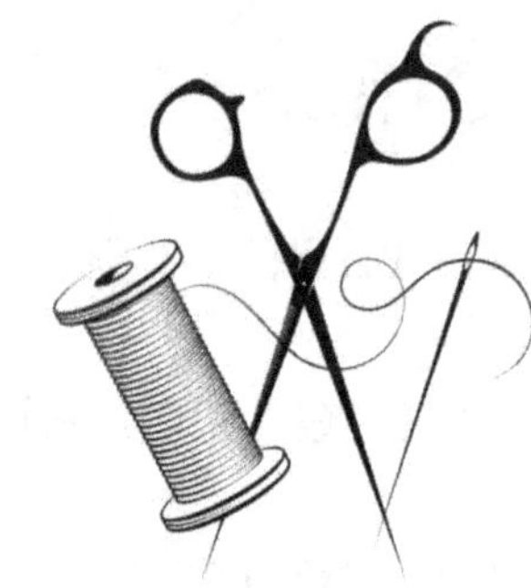

Reflection & Notes:
- Did simplicity make it stronger?
- Which element carried the look?
- What would I adjust?

Pro Tip: Minimalism lets structure and form shine.

Outfit Inspiration: Streetwear

Layered Streetwear

Layering is a way to turn basics into something dynamic. A t-shirt under a hoodie, topped with a bomber or denim jacket, instantly creates depth. Mixing fabrics – cotton, denim, nylon – makes outfits feel three-dimensional.

The trick with layering is balance. Too many bulky layers can overwhelm, but 2–3 pieces styled with intention create richness and flexibility.

Pro Tip: Use layering to experiment with color. Pair neutrals with one bright shade – for example, a neutral hoodie under a colorful jacket – to create controlled contrast.

Trends

Inspiration

Textiles

Notes

Details

Swatches

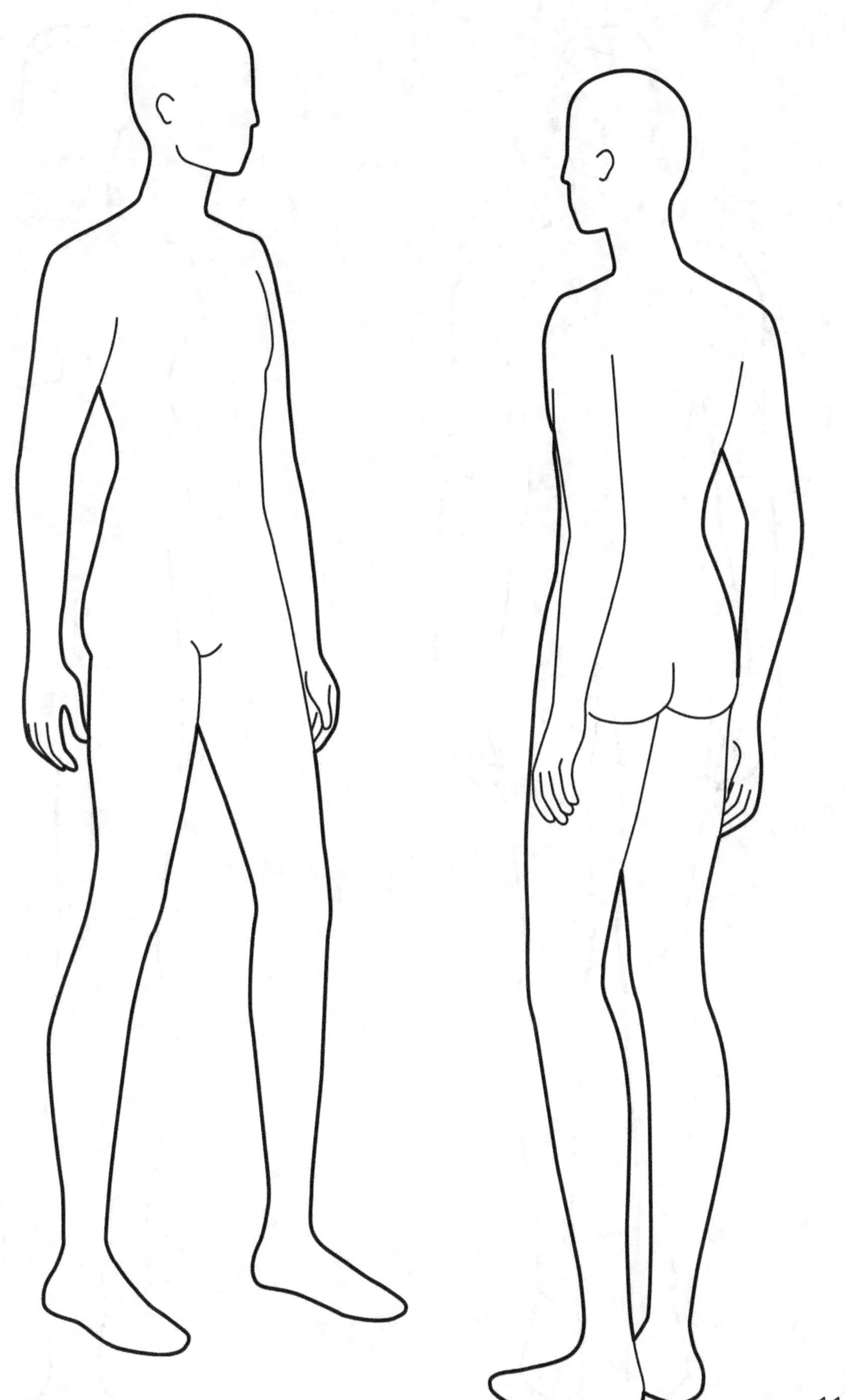

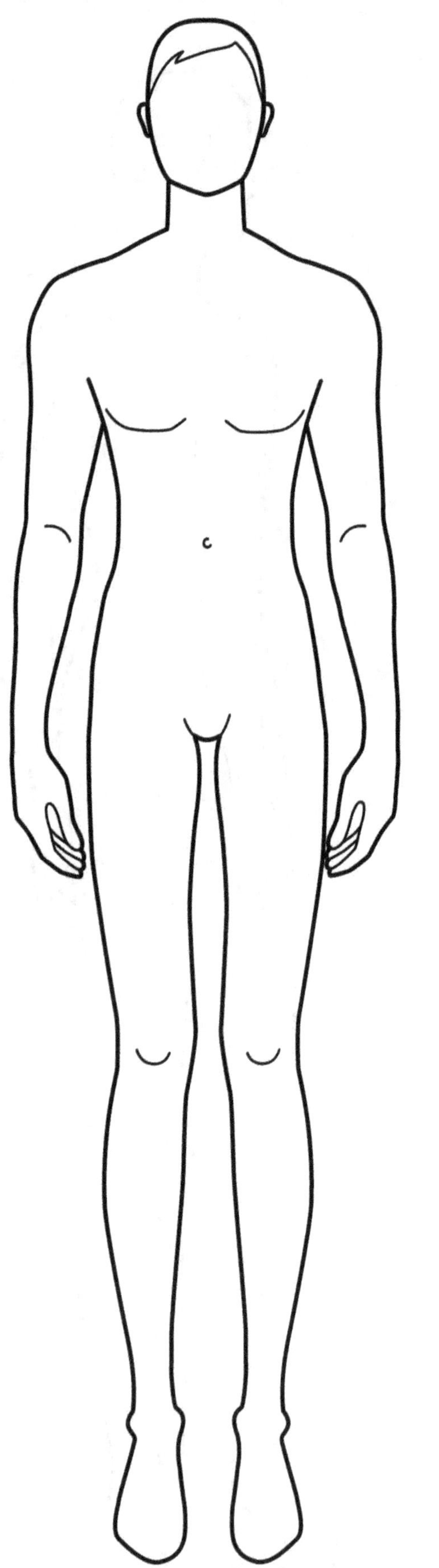
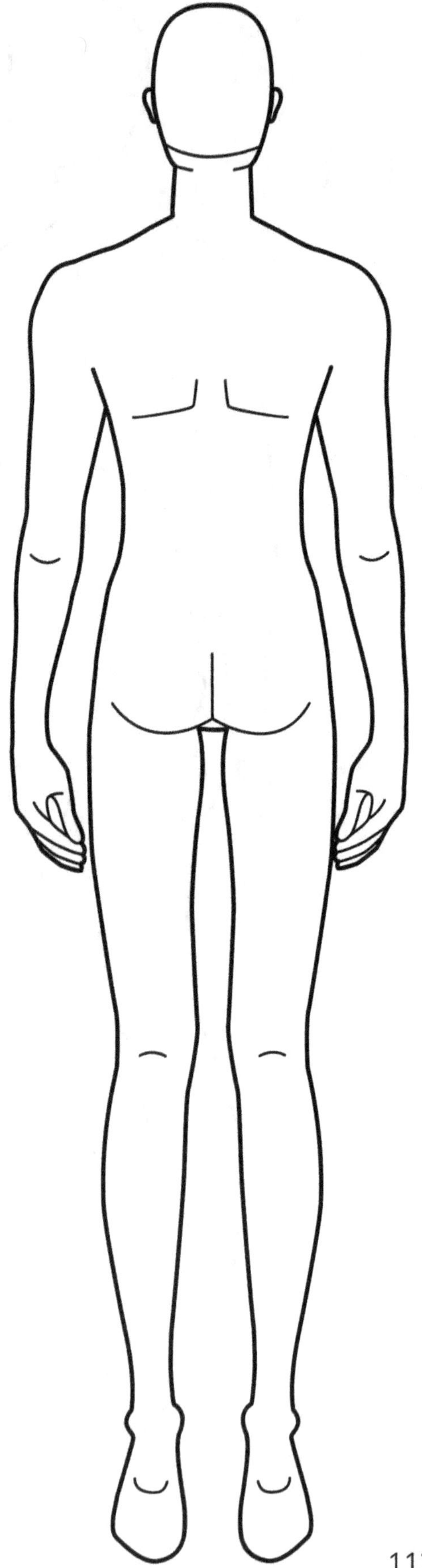

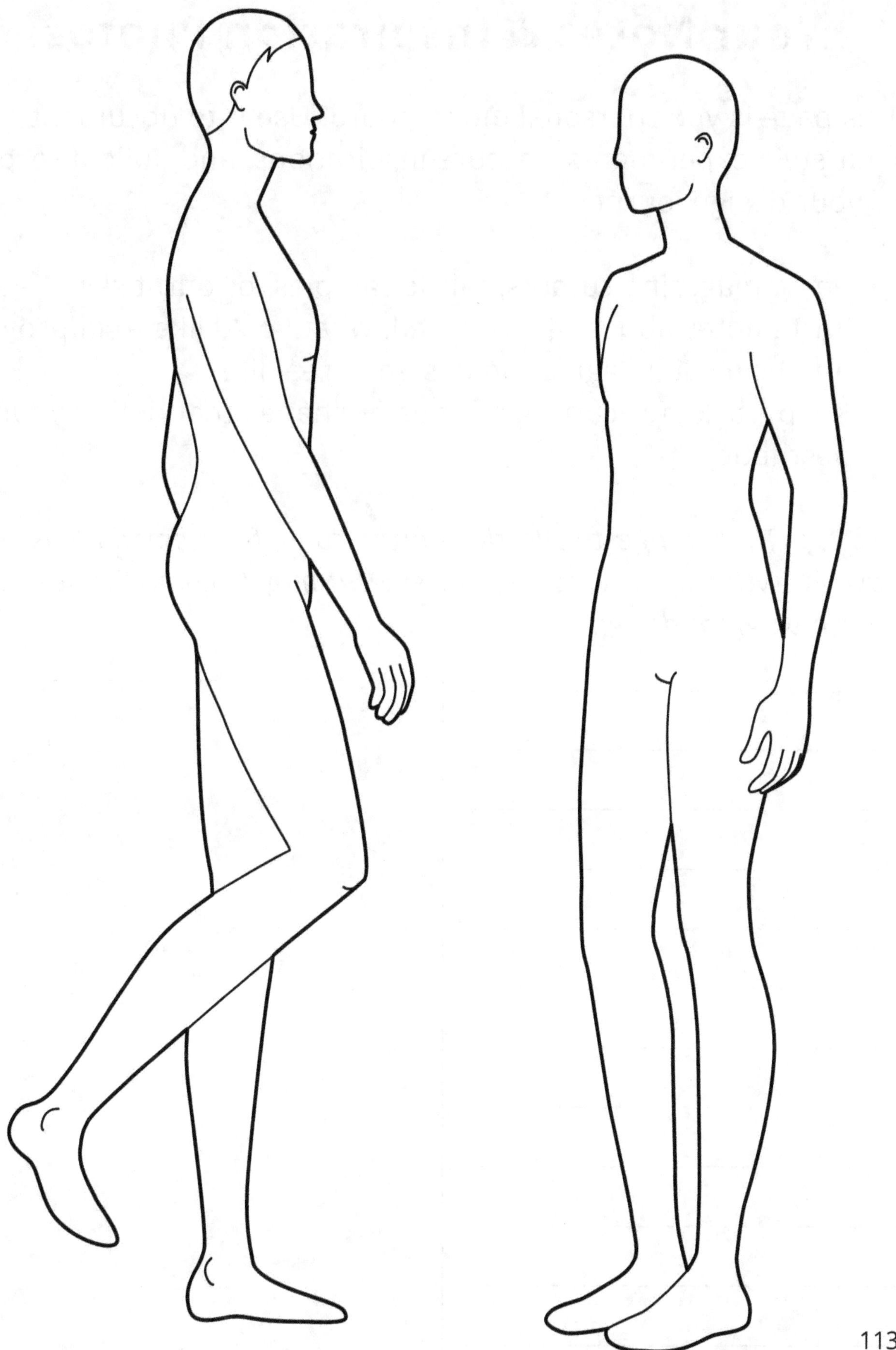

113

Your Notes & Inspiration Photos

This page is your personal mood board. Use it to document your style experiments, capture inspirations, and build a record of your design journey.

- Paste magazine cutouts, fabric samples, or outfit sketches.
- Write notes about what worked, what you'd like to improve, and how you imagine the design in real life.
- Keep track of recurring themes or shapes that define your aesthetic.

Pro Tip: *The strongest collections often come from small ideas. Save everything that catches your eye – it may become the seed of your next great design.*

Outfit Inspiration: Office Chic and Runway Glam

Relaxed Tailoring + Red Carpet Classic

Office Chic Inspiration

Relaxed tailoring balances comfort with style. Soft-structured blazers paired with pleated trousers and loafers project ease without sacrificing professionalism. Lighter fabrics like linen or cotton blends adapt to different climates while staying chic.

Runway Glam Inspiration

Classic red carpet glam for men centers around timeless tuxedos or three-piece suits. Velvet jackets, silk lapels, and bow ties emphasize luxury. Polished shoes and elegant grooming complete the refined aesthetic.

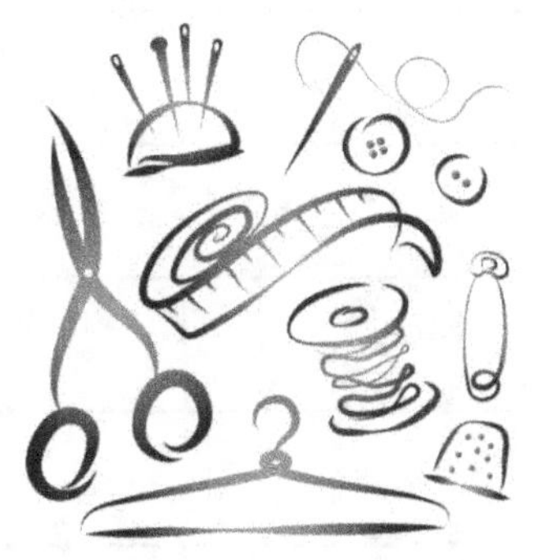

Fashion Practice Guide & Notes

This page is for reflection and progress. Look at your past sketches and celebrate improvement.

How to Use This Page:
- Sketch one outfit that shows your growth.
- Write what you've learned so far.
- Set one design challenge for next time.

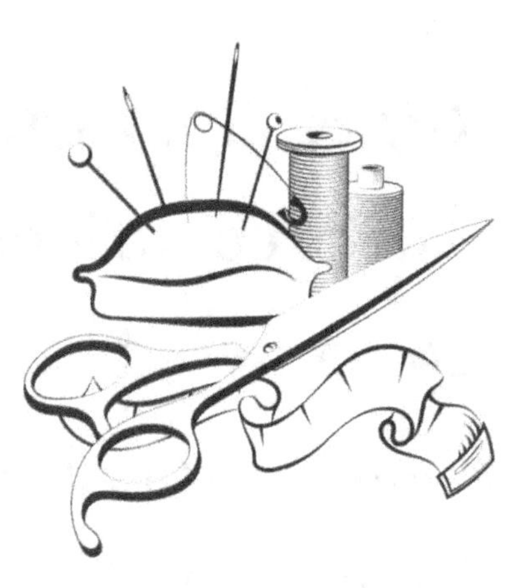

Reflection & Notes:
- What improved most?
- Which technique needs more work?
- What's my next goal?

Pro Tip: *Every sketch is a milestone in your journey.*

____

____

____

____

____

____

____

____

Outfit Inspiration: Streetwear

Retro Streetwear

Retro streetwear pulls from the '80s and '90s: track jackets, color-block windbreakers, oversized sneakers, and snapbacks.

It's nostalgic yet still on-trend. Vintage-inspired designs connect the past with today's street scene, making the outfit playful but still stylish.

The secret to pulling off retro looks is moderation. Mixing one retro piece with modern basics keeps it fresh and avoids looking like a costume.

Pro Tip: Choose one standout retro item – like a bold track jacket – and keep the rest of the outfit contemporary. That balance creates authenticity with a modern twist.

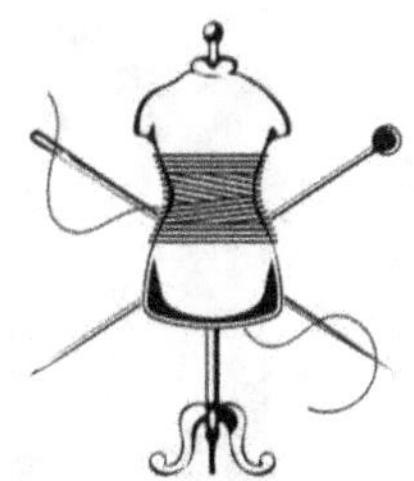

Trends

Inspiration

Textiles

Notes

Details

Swatches

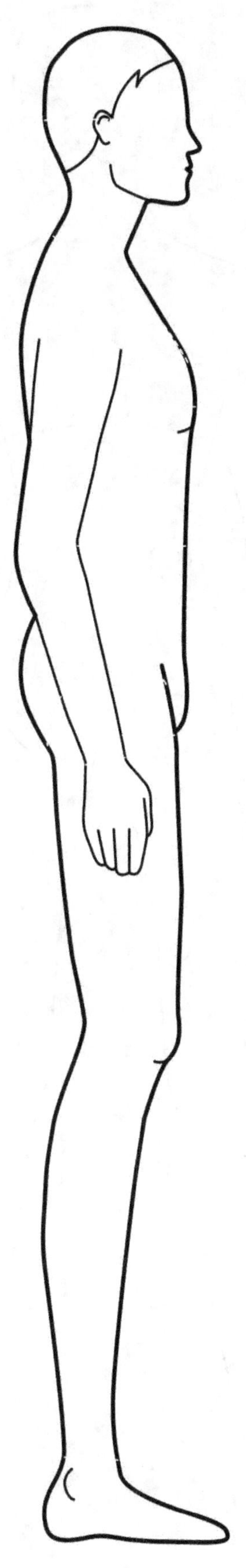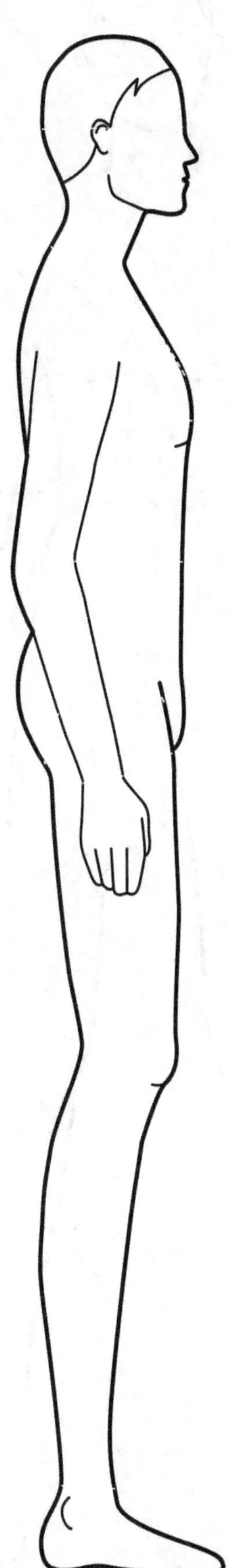

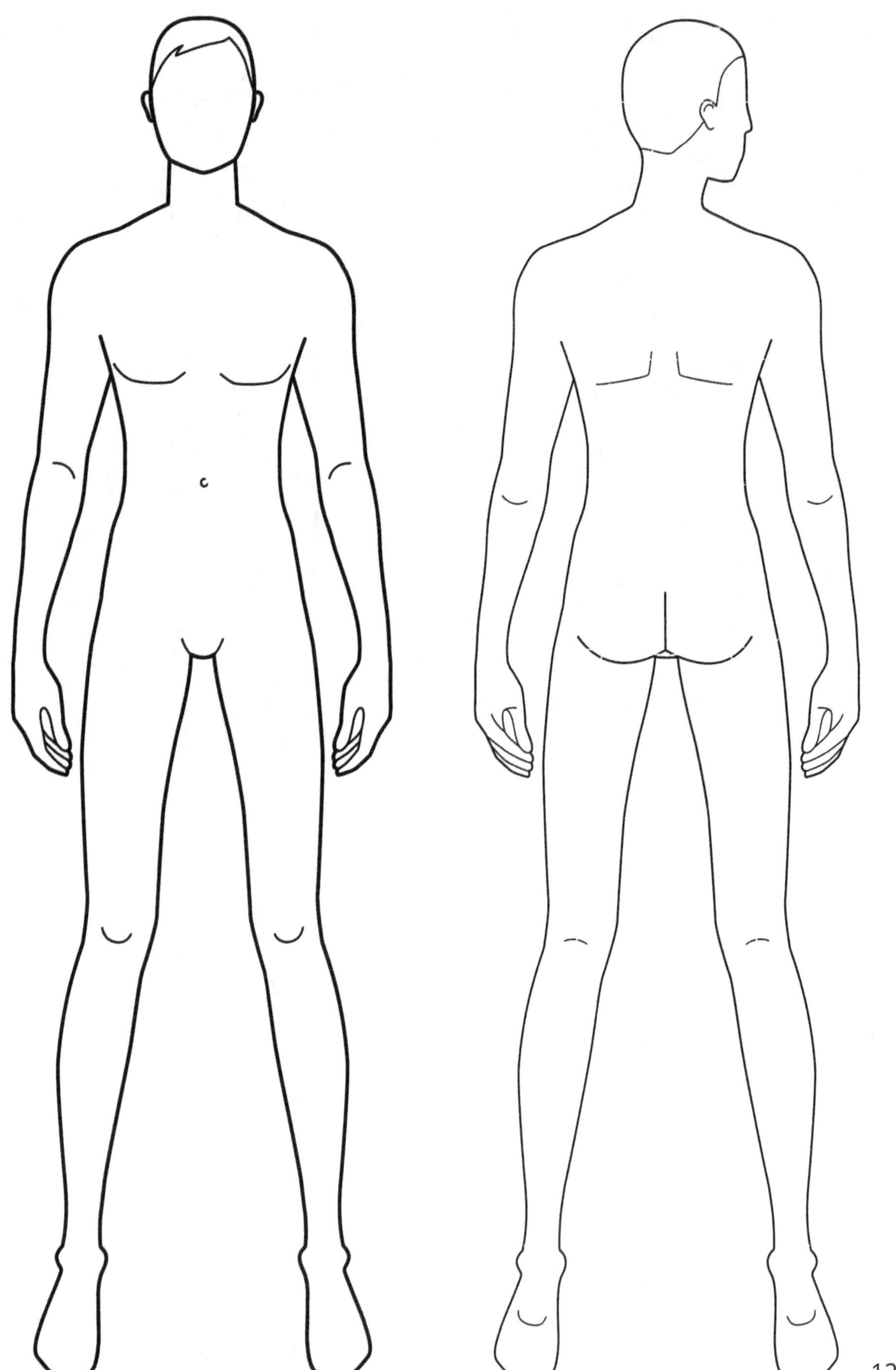

This page is your personal mood board. Use it to document your style experiments, capture inspirations, and build a record of your design journey.

- Paste magazine cutouts, fabric samples, or outfit sketches.
- Write notes about what worked, what you'd like to improve, and how you imagine the design in real life.
- Keep track of recurring themes or shapes that define your aesthetic.

Pro Tip: *The strongest collections often come from small ideas. Save everything that catches your eye – it may become the seed of your next great design.*

Outfit Inspiration:
Office Chic and Runway Glam

Bold Statement Look + Avant-Garde Menswear

Office Chic Inspiration

Sometimes office wear is about making a statement. Boldly colored blazers, patterned shirts, or unexpected textures elevate daily outfits. Pairing these with neutral trousers balances creativity with professionalism.

Runway Glam Inspiration

Avant-garde menswear explores dramatic silhouettes and experimental fabrics. Oversized coats, asymmetrical tailoring, or layered textures challenge convention. These designs are meant to captivate audiences, merging conceptual art with fashion.

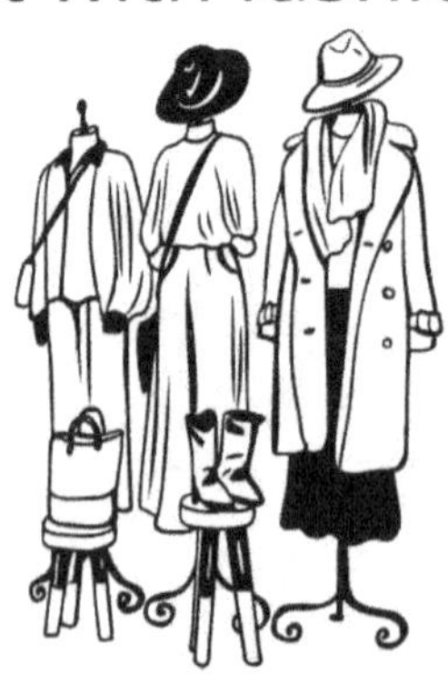

Trends

Inspiration

Textiles

Notes

Details

Swatches

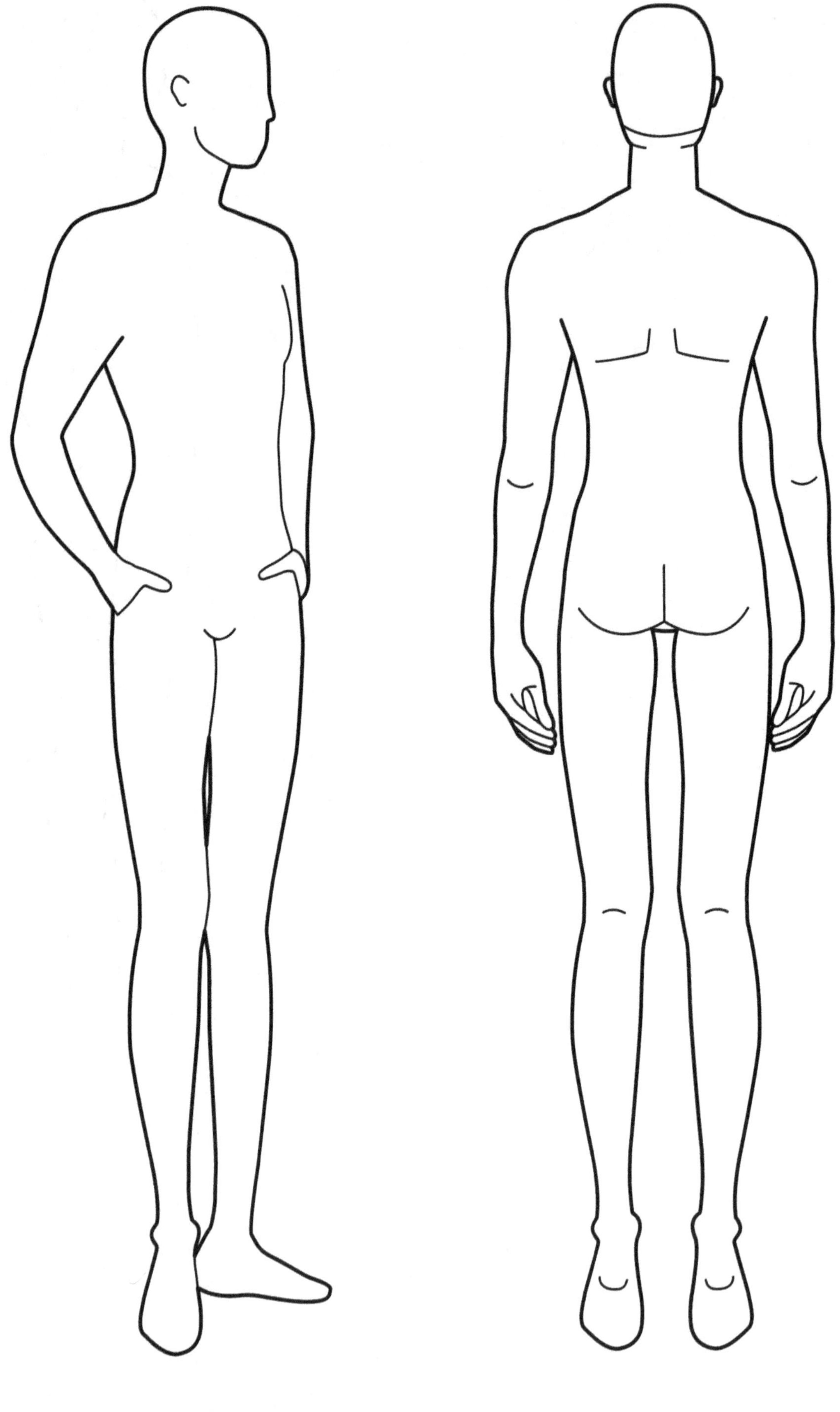

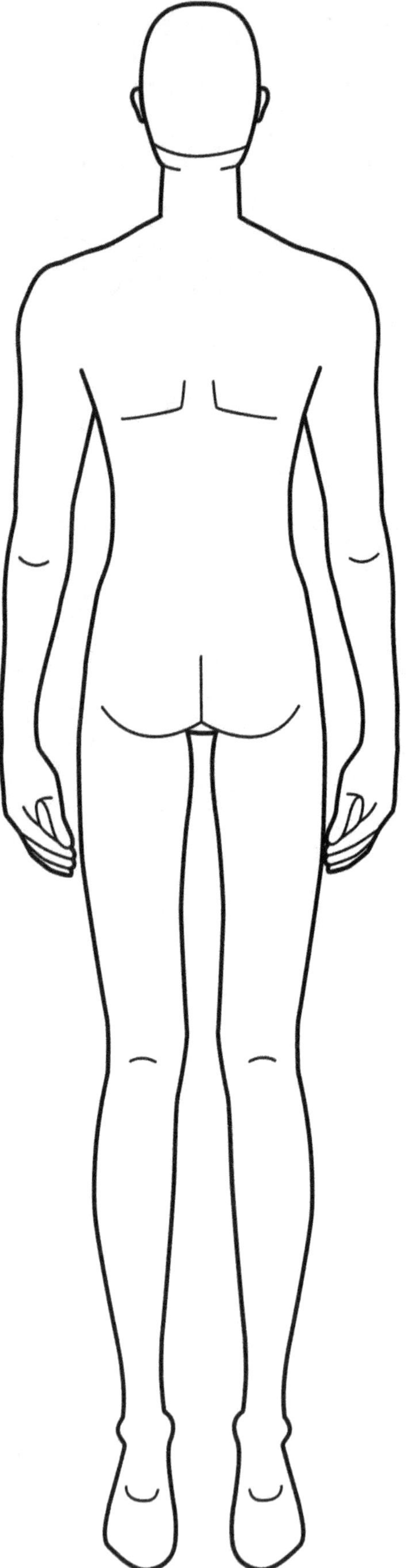

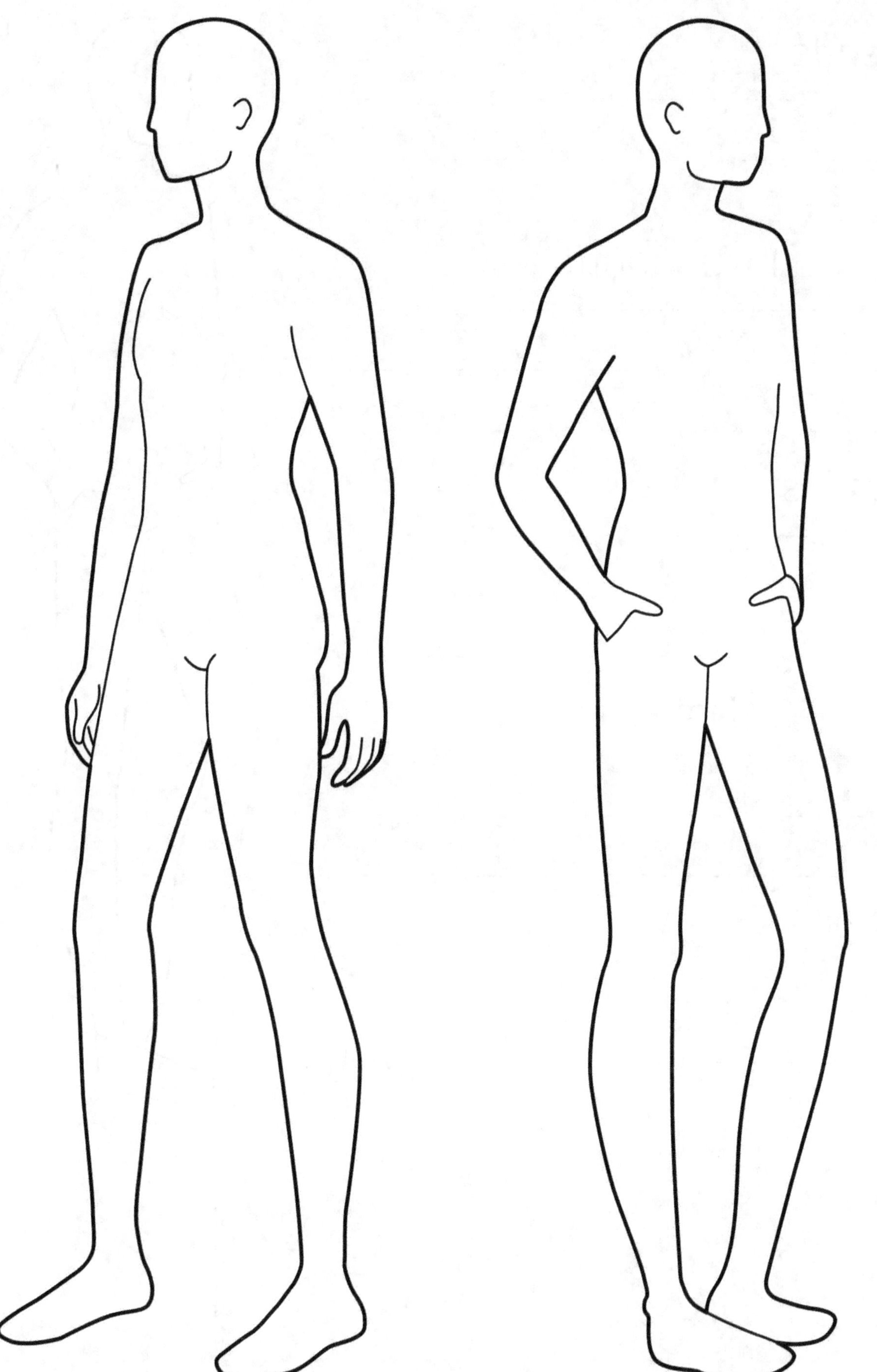

Trends

Inspiration

Textiles

Notes

Details

Swatches

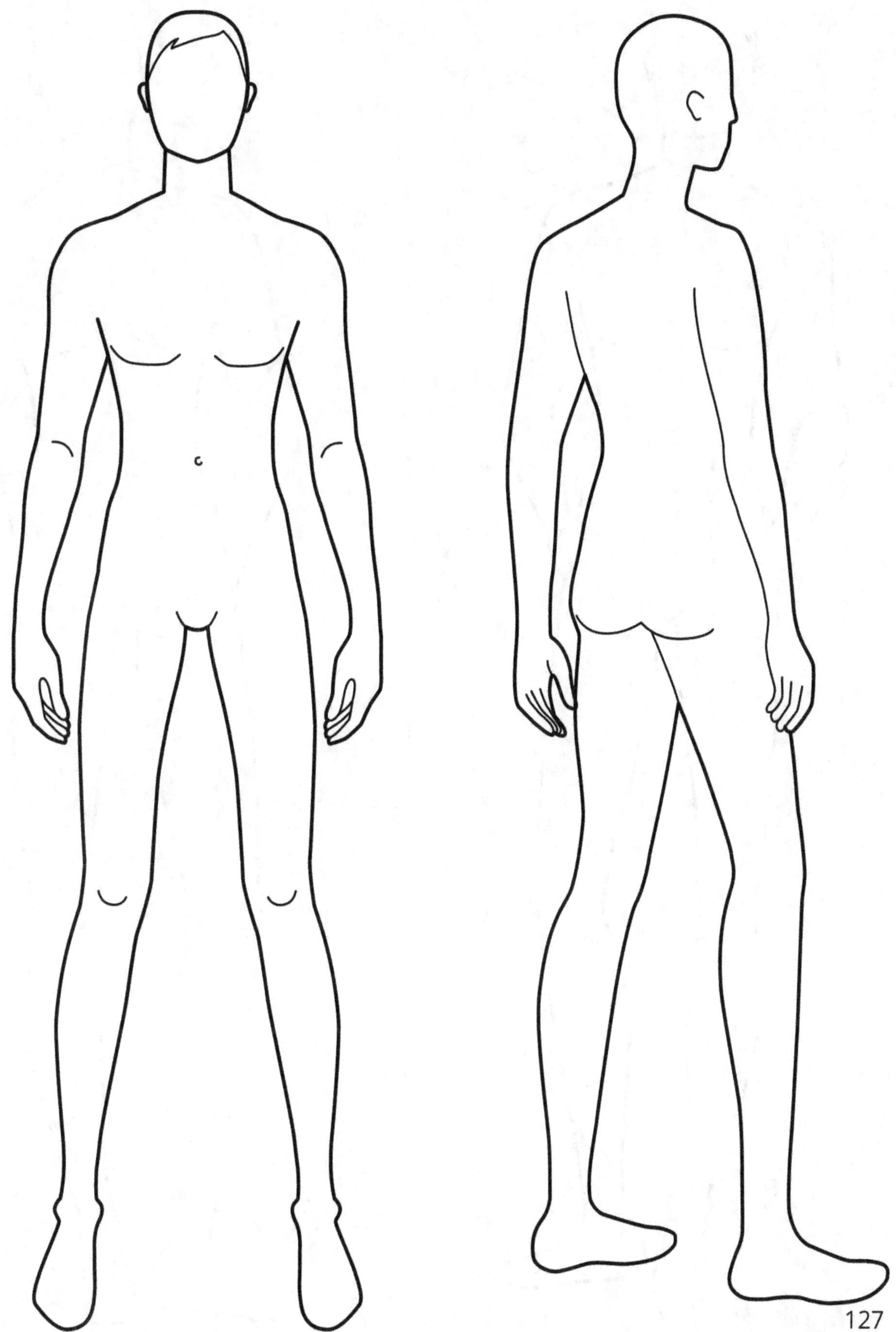

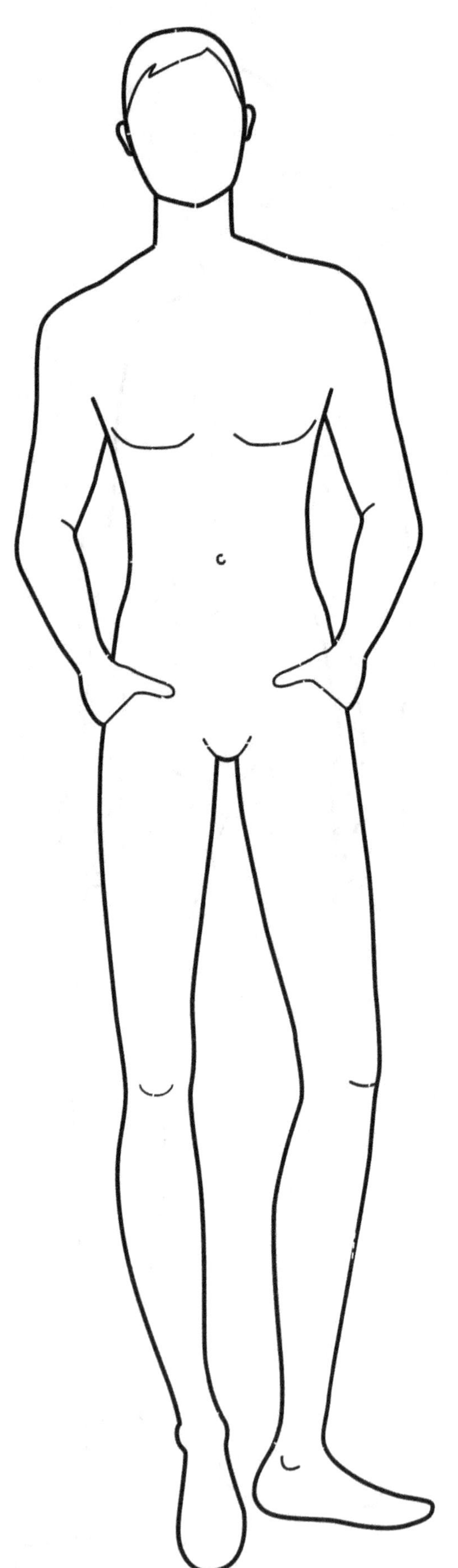
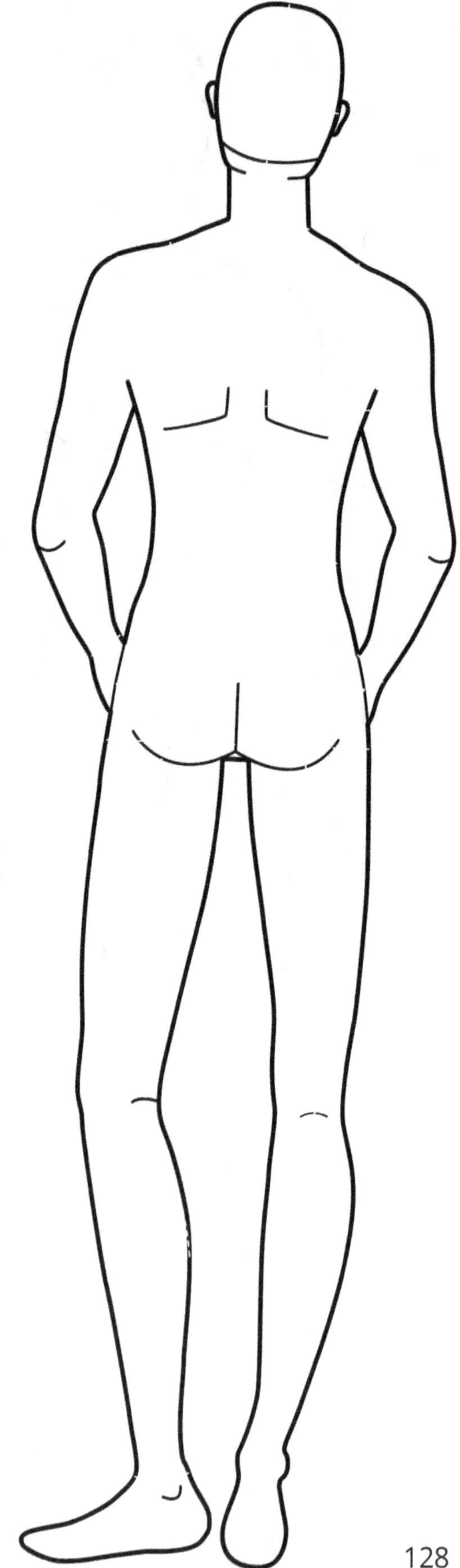

Trends

Inspiration

Textiles

Notes

Details

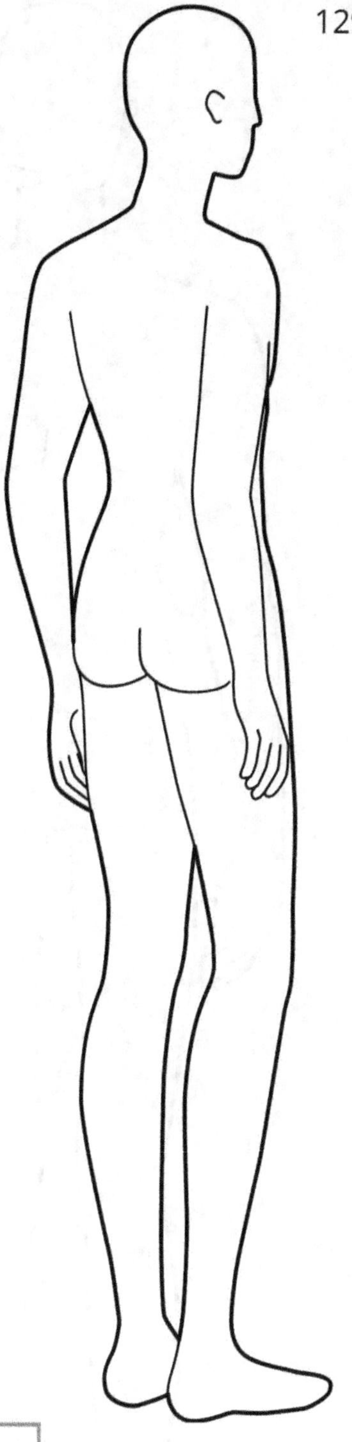

Swatches

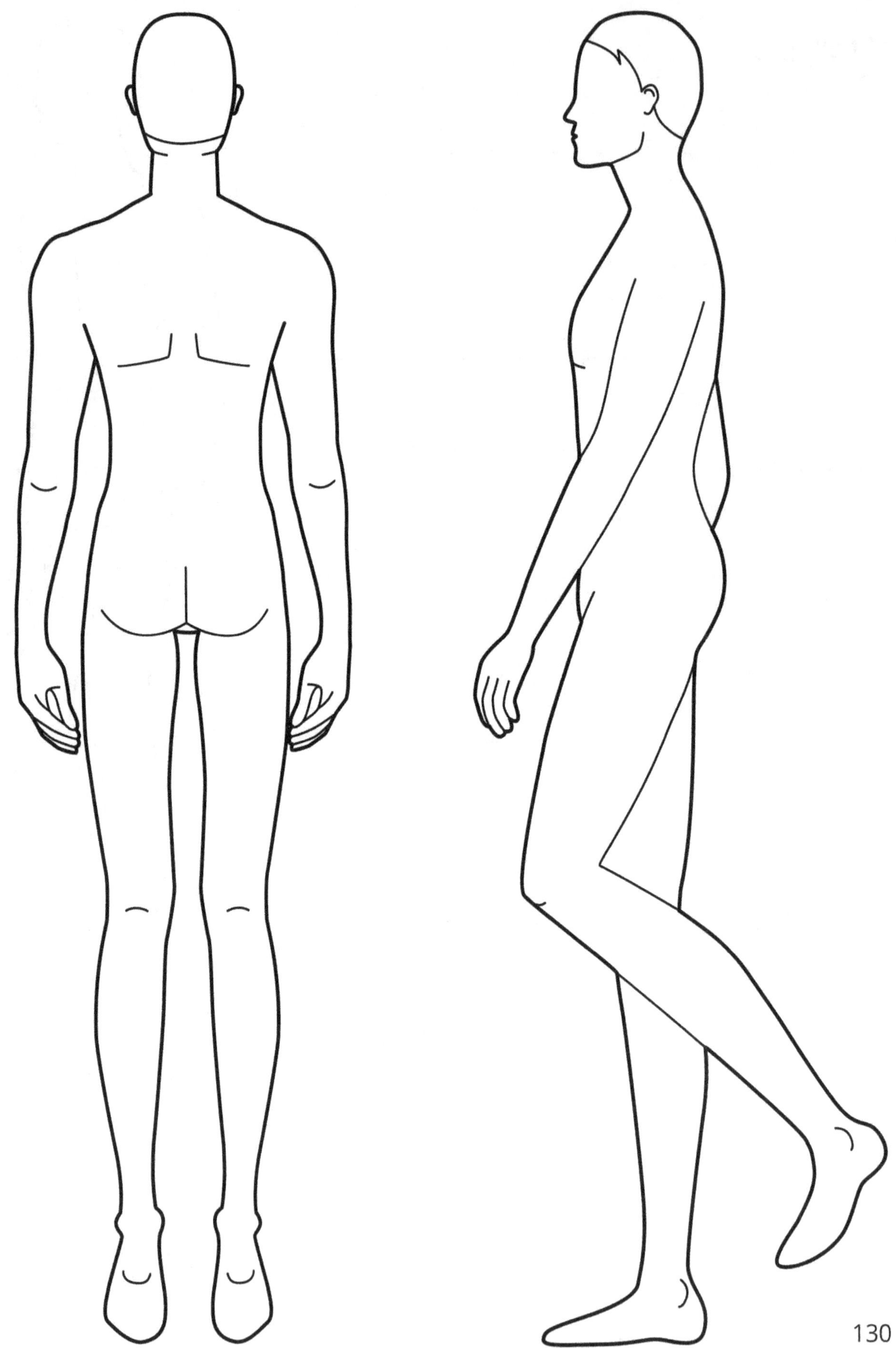

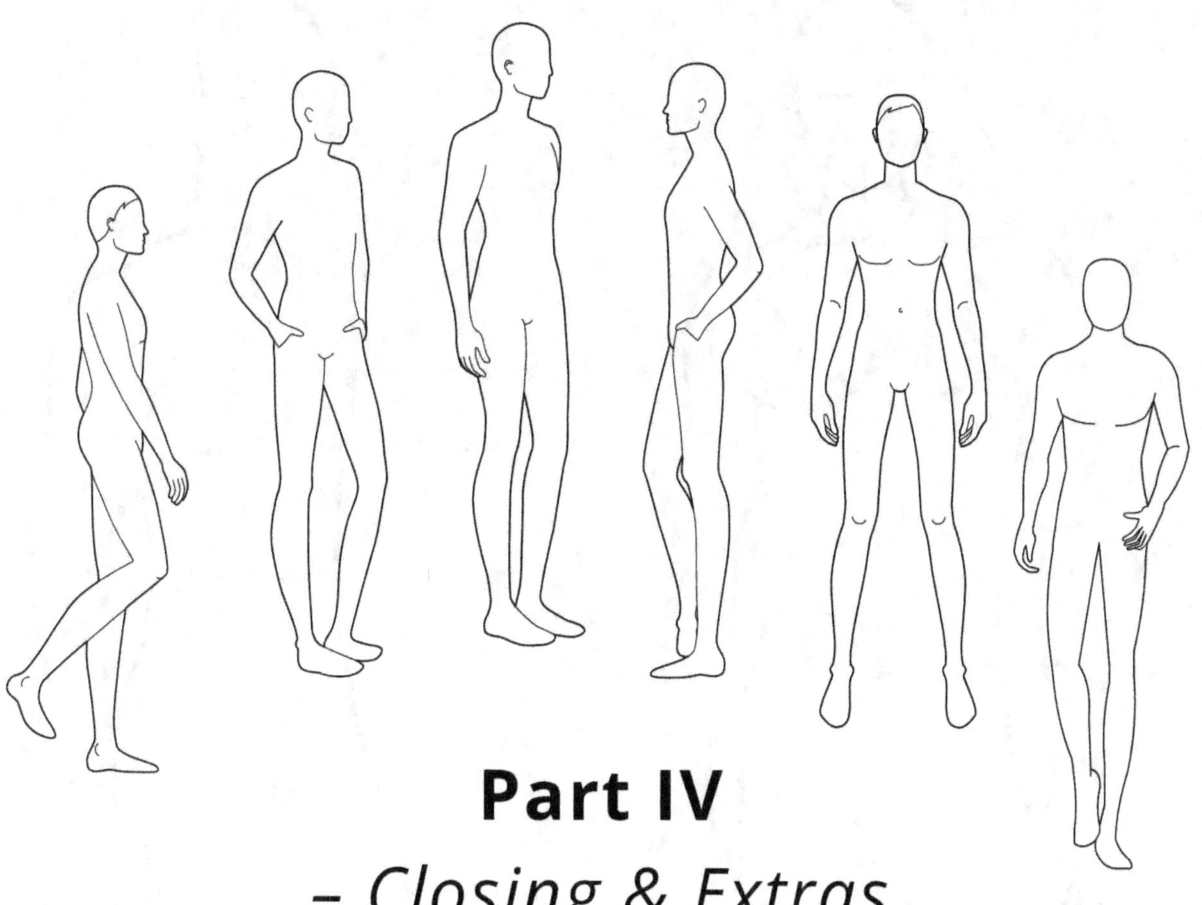

Part IV

– Closing & Extras

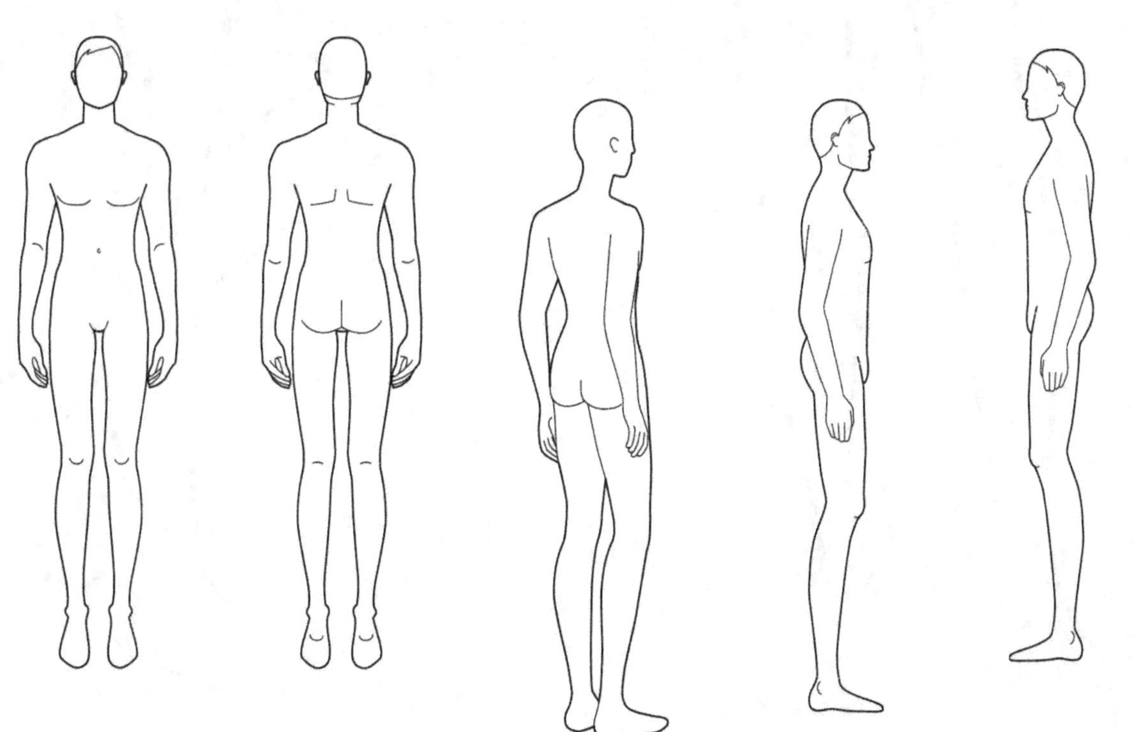

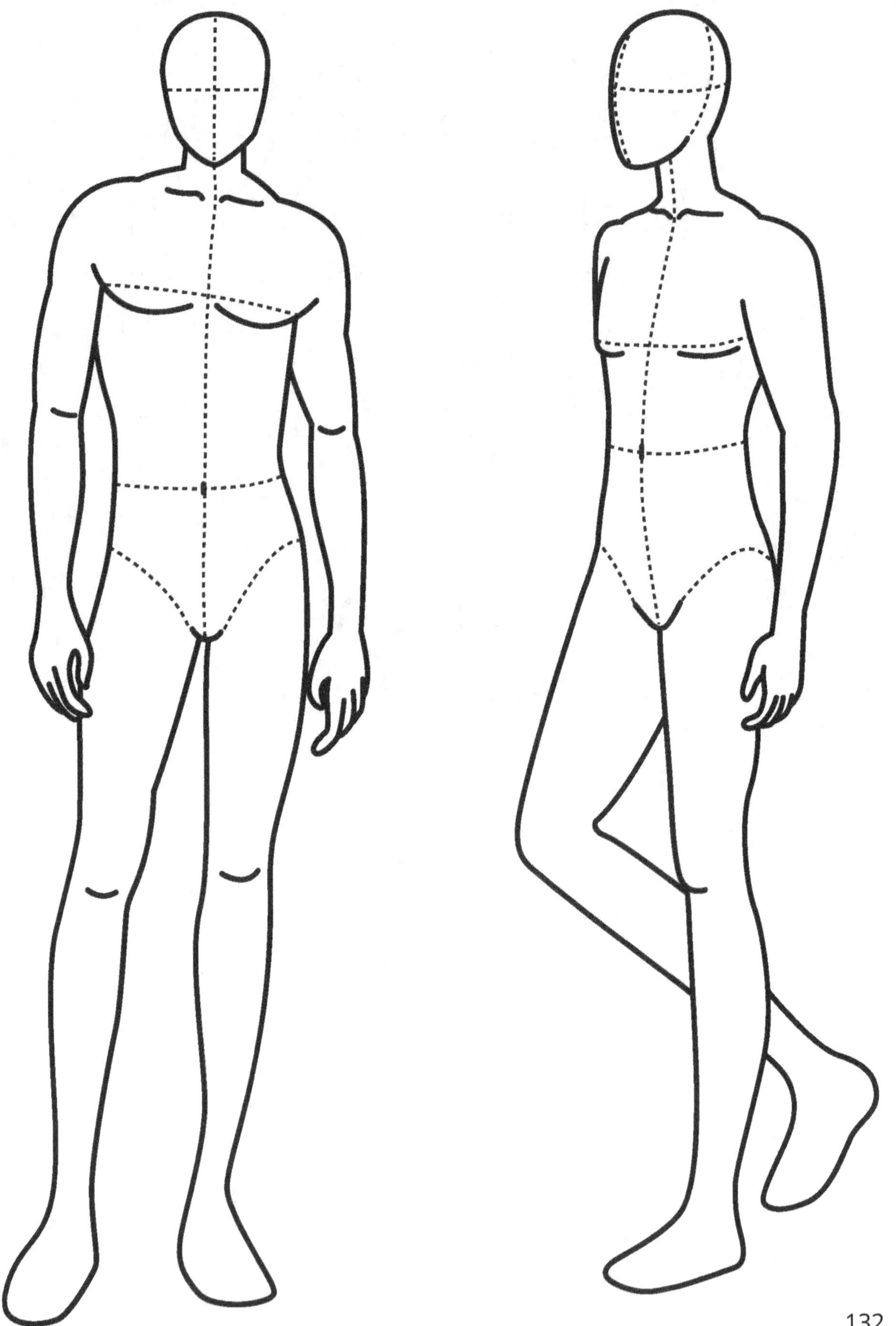

Redesign a Classic Silhouette

Take a timeless men's silhouette-such as a tailored suit, bomber jacket, or denim jeans-and give it a modern twist. Keep the structure but experiment with fabric, color, or detail.

Prompts:
- Which part of the design did you change the most?
- Did you keep it wearable or make it more artistic?
- How does your redesign speak to today's trends?

Pro Tip: *"Modern updates breathe life into classics."*

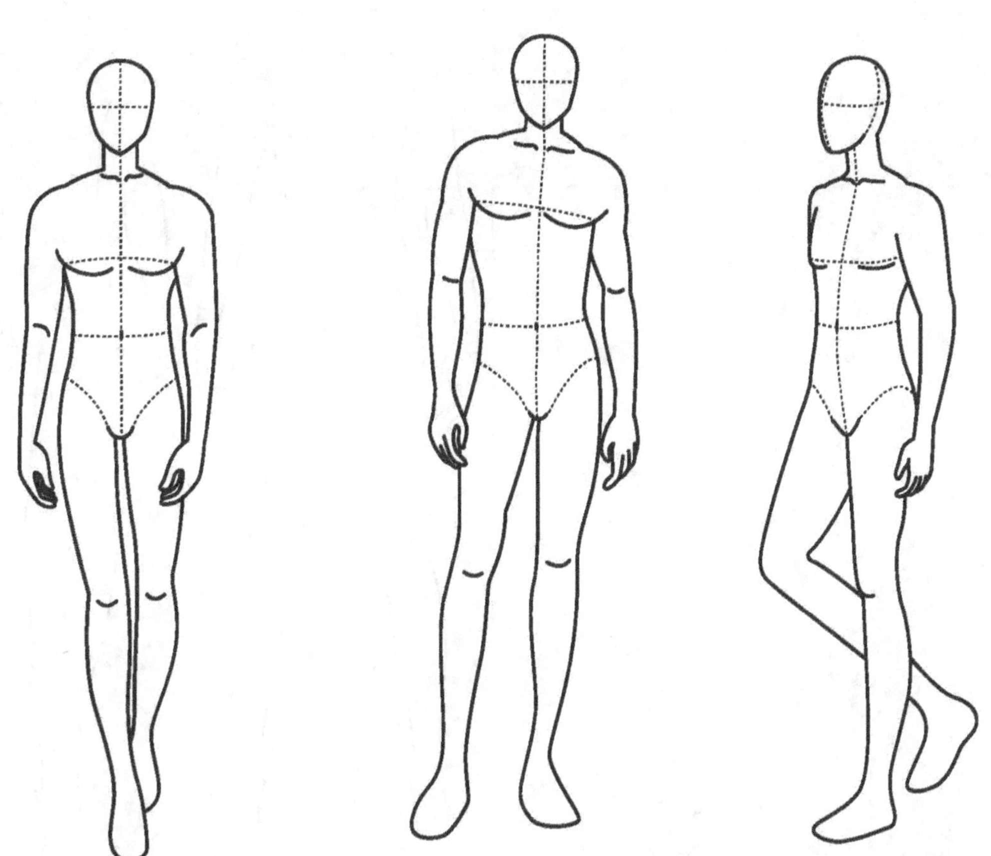

Capsule Wardrobe Challenge

Design a capsule wardrobe of 5 essential men's outfits. Focus on versatility: each piece should mix and match with the others.

Prompts:
- Which 5 items form the foundation of your capsule?
- How do they work together to cover different occasions?
- Is the balance between casual and formal well thought out?

Pro Tip: *"Less pieces, more possibilities."*

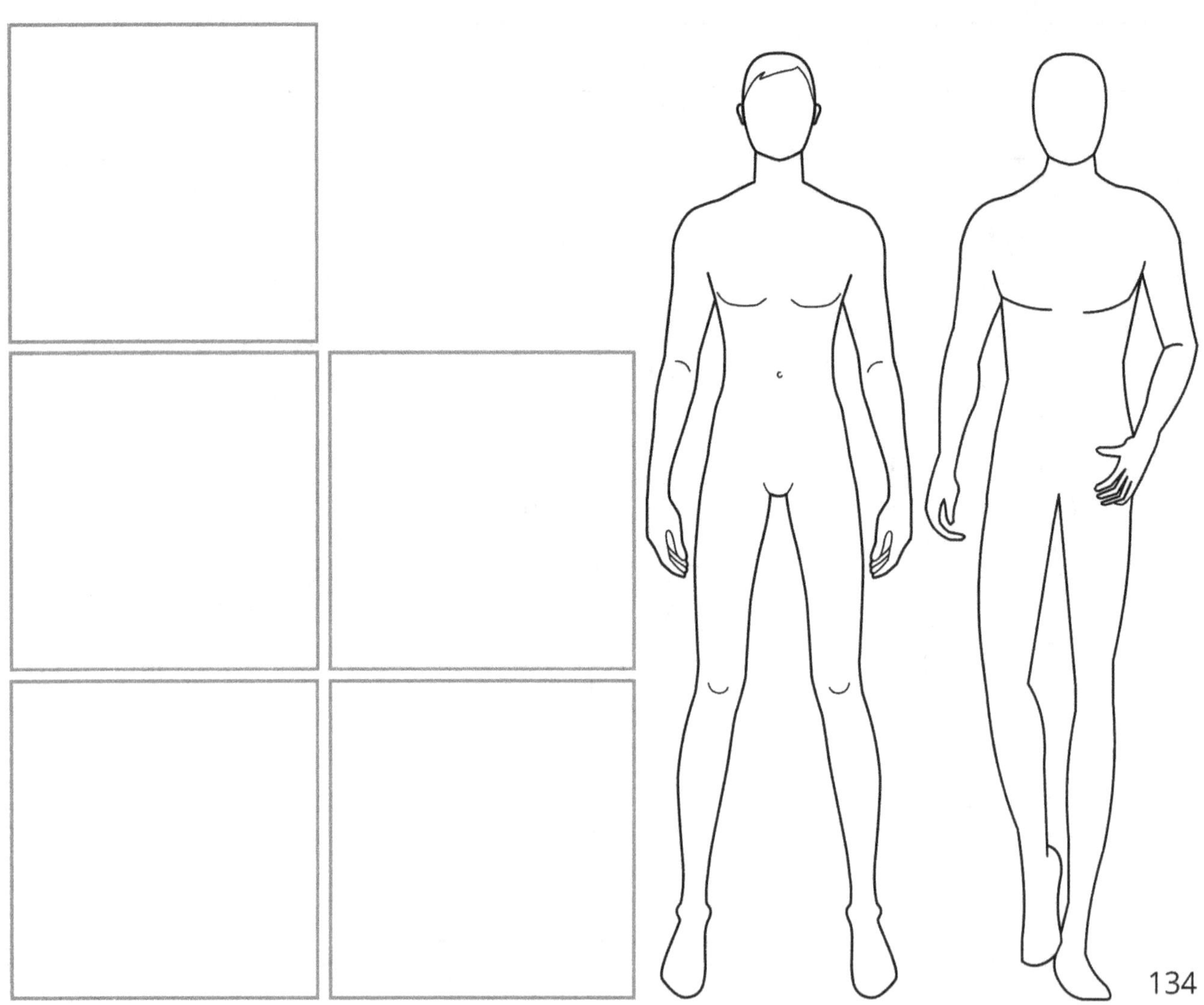

Seasonal Inspiration

Choose a season and create an outfit inspired by it-spring freshness, summer ease, autumn layering, or winter elegance.

Prompts:
- Which colors or textures best represent your season?
- How does functionality (warmth, comfort, breathability) play into your design?
- Does the outfit still feel stylish and current?

Pro Tip: *"Seasonal style = timeless inspiration."*

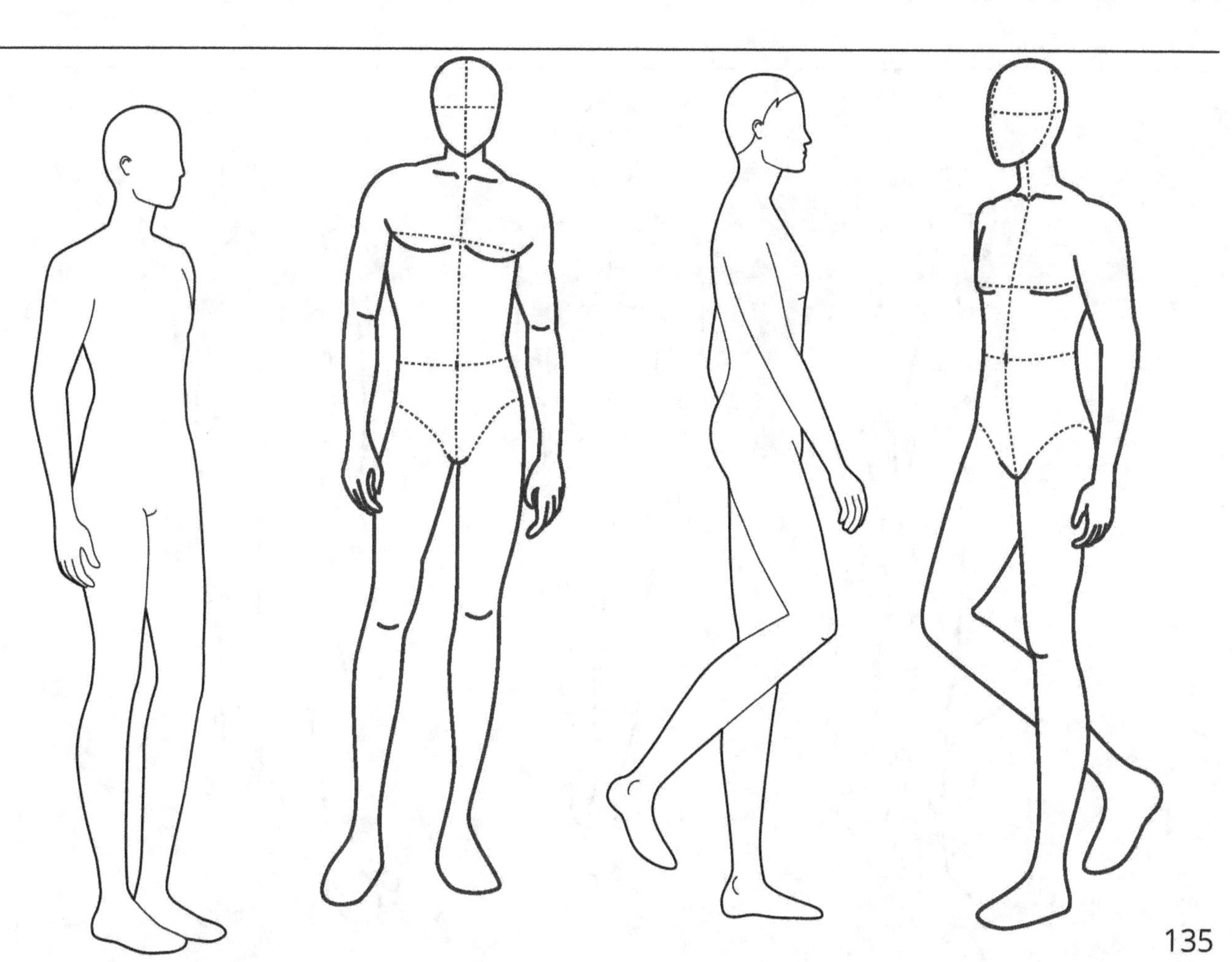

T-shirt Transformation

Start with a plain men's T-shirt and reinvent it. Play with cuts, graphics, layering, or material combinations.

Prompts:
- How does your T-shirt stand out from the ordinary?
- Is it more casual, sporty, or high-fashion?
- Would your design work for mass production or as a limited edition?

Pro Tip: *"The simplest item can carry the boldest ideas."*

____

____

____

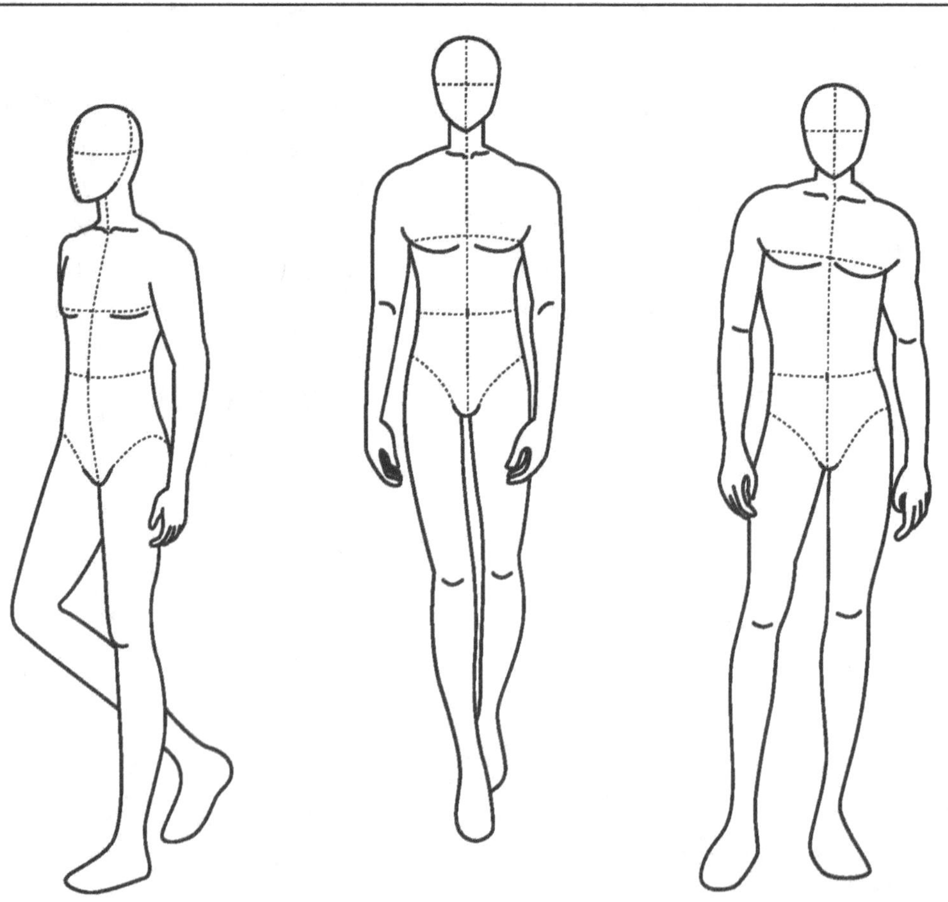

Mix & Match Opposites

Combine two opposing styles in one outfit (ex: streetwear + formal, sporty + luxury, vintage + futuristic).

Prompts:
- Which elements contrast most strongly?
- How did you balance tension and harmony?
- Is the result unexpected but wearable?

Pro Tip: *"Contrasts create character."*

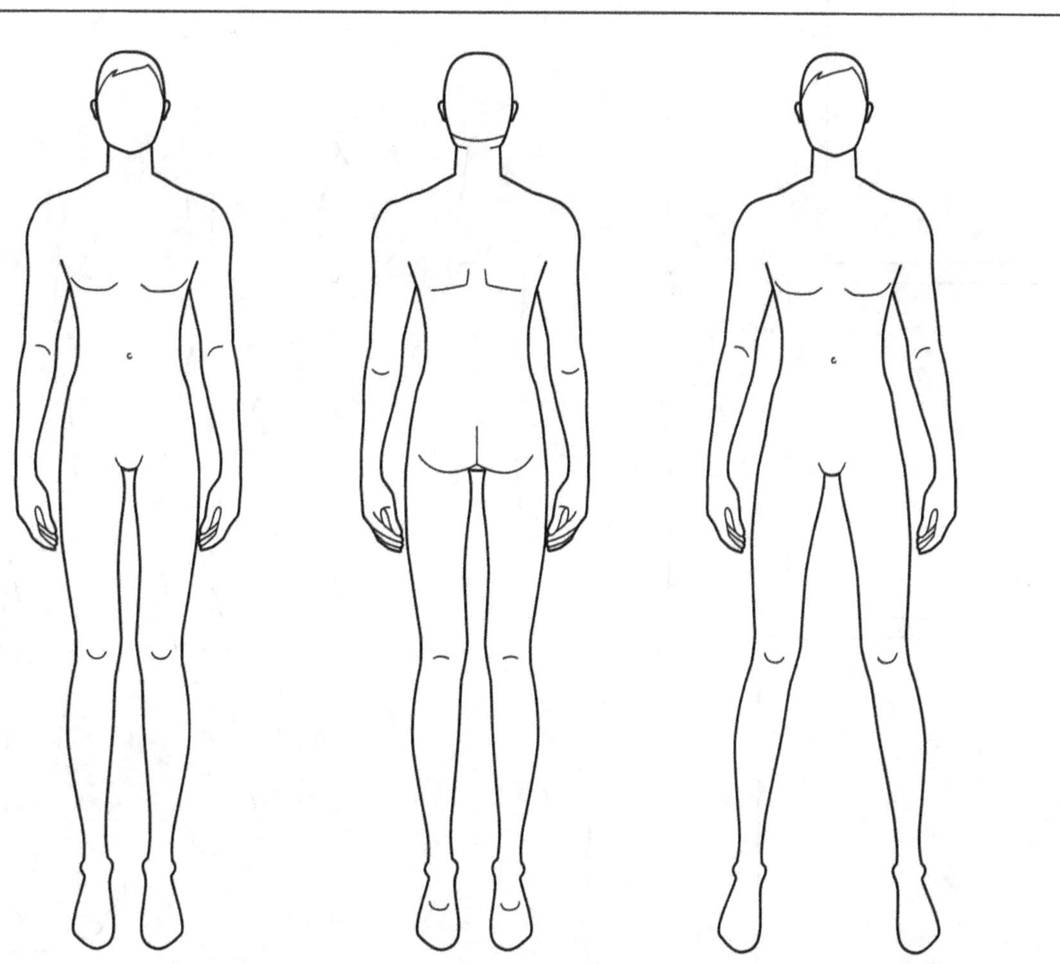

Accessory Focus

Design a statement men's accessory (watch, sneakers, backpack, hat, tie, etc.) that transforms a look. Accessories tell powerful stories.

Prompts:
- Which accessory did you choose and why?
- How does it complement or elevate the outfit?
- Could it become a signature piece in a collection?

Pro Tip: *"Accessories are the exclamation points of style."*

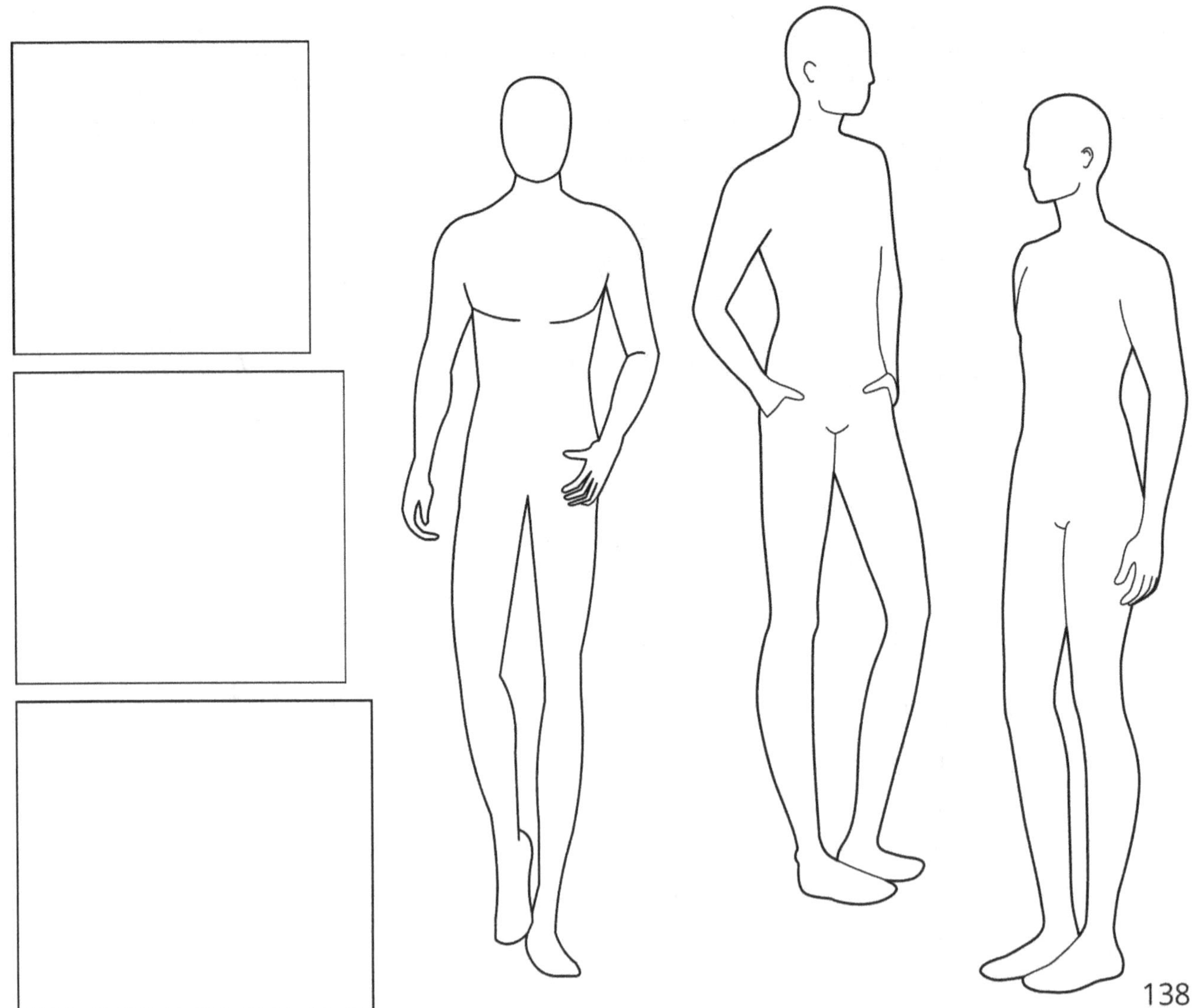

Fashion Through Time

Pick a decade (1920s, 1970s, 1990s, etc.) and redesign a men's look inspired by that era, but updated for today.

Prompts:
- Which key elements define your chosen decade?
- How did you adapt them to modern trends?
- Does the design keep its retro charm while feeling current?

Pro Tip: *"Every decade leaves a mark-reinterpret it with your vision."*

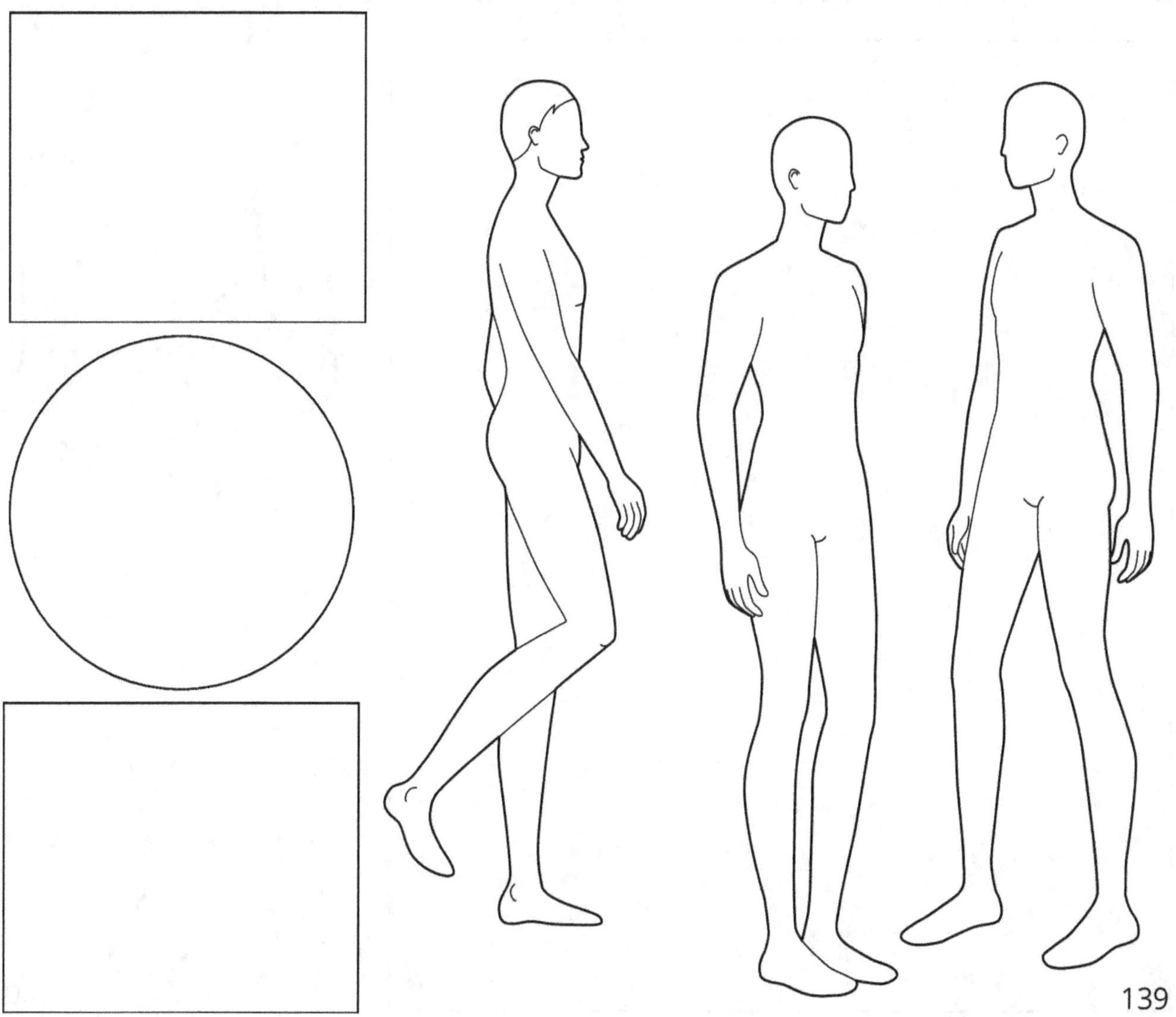

Moodboard to Outfit

Create a mini moodboard and then design an outfit based on it. Gather colors, textures, and images that inspire you, paste or draw them in the space below, and then translate that feeling into a wearable look.

Prompts:
- What's the theme of your moodboard?
- Which elements translated into your design?
- Does the final outfit 'feel' like your board?

Pro Tip*: "A strong concept = a strong collection."*

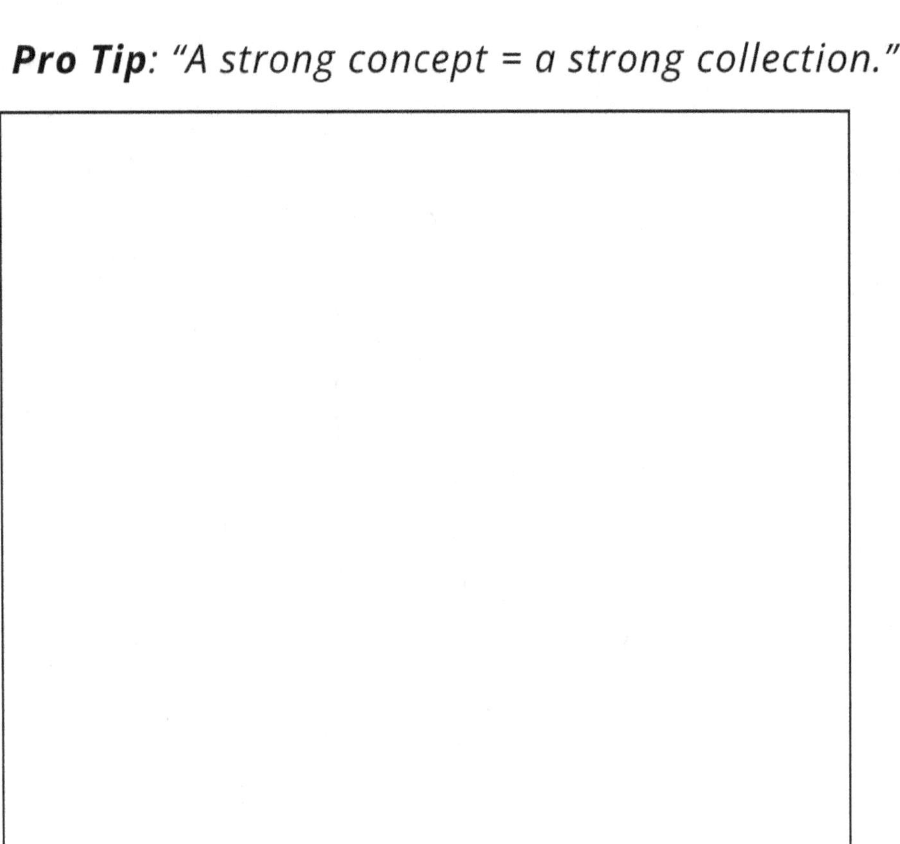

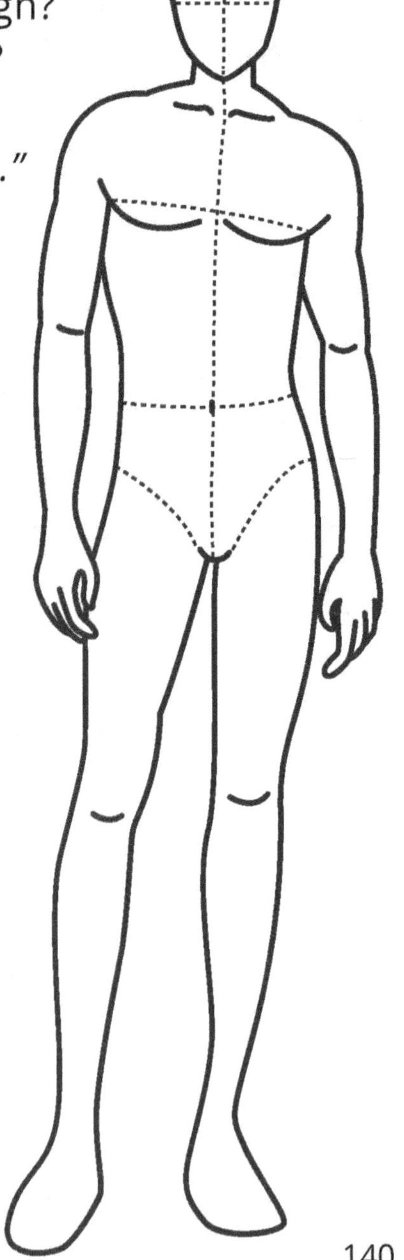

Fashion Designer Checklist

Every fashion designer needs the right tools and essentials. Use this checklist to stay prepared for every sketching session and design project. Tick the boxes as you build your creative toolkit, and feel free to add your own must-haves!

Essentials for Designing
- Sketchbooks & Blank Paper ....
- Fashion Figure Templates ....
- Pencils (HB, 2B, 4B) ....
- Fine Liners & Ink Pens ....
- Erasers & Sharpeners ....
- Rulers & French Curves ....

Color & Textures
- Color Pencils ....
- Markers / Alcohol Markers ....
- Watercolors or Gouache ....
- Fabric Swatches ....
- Texture Samples ....

Tools & Accessories
- Scissors & Cutters ....
- Glue Stick / Tape ....
- Measuring Tape ....
- Pins / Clips ....
- Portfolio Folder ....

Digital Tools (Optional)
- Drawing Tablet ....
- Stylus Pen ....
- Fashion Software (CAD / Sketch Apps) ....

Fabric Research
- Textile Catalogs ....
- Trend Magazines ....
- Moodboard Materials ....

My Favorite Fabrics & Brands
– Space for Notes

This page is just for you! Write down your favorite fabrics, textures, and go-to brands. Think about materials that inspire you most - whether it's soft cotton, structured wool, or sleek leather.

- My Top 3 Fabrics:
- Fabrics I'd Love to Work With:
- My Go-To Textile Store/Brand:
- Fabric That Represents My Style:
- Dream Material to Use in the Future:

Leave space for notes and small boxes for fabric swatches or taped samples.

____

____

____

____

____

____

____

____

____

My Personal Fashion Journal

A space for your reflections as a designer.

You've reached the final section of this sketchbook-but this is only the beginning of your creative journey. Use this page to capture your thoughts, lessons, and dreams:

- What I've learned so far:
- My favorite designs I created:
- The style that best represents me:
- Next goals as a designer:

"Every sketch is a new possibility. Keep experimenting, keep sketching, keep creating."

____

____

____

____

____

____

____

____

____

____

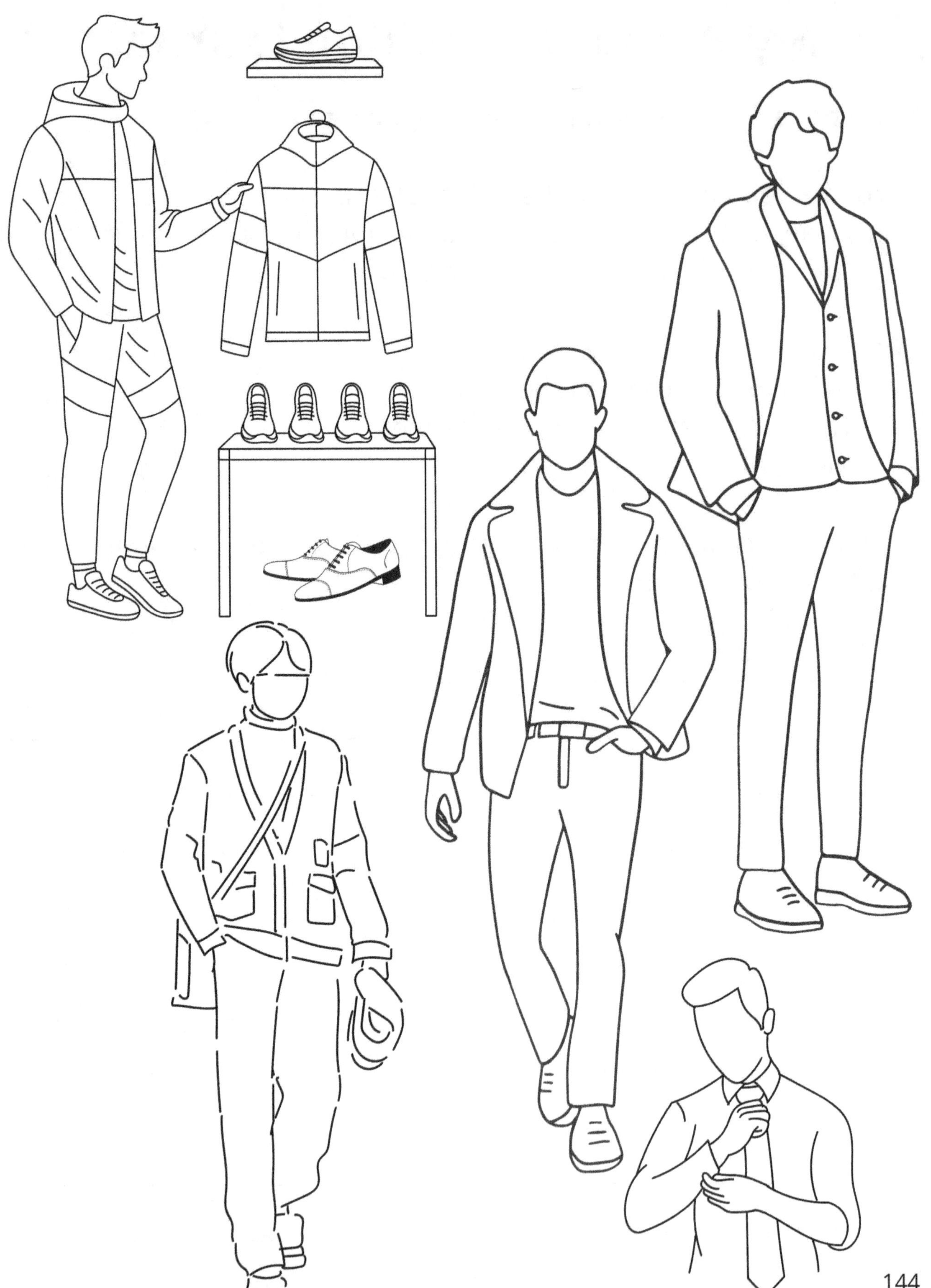

Congratulations!
You Did It!

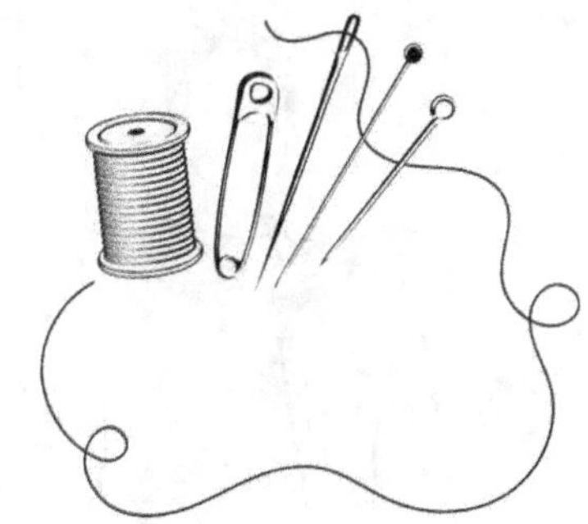

Congratulations, Designer!

You've reached the last pages of this practice book, which means you've invested time, energy, and creativity into developing your vision. Whether you started as a beginner or already had experience, every sketch, idea, and note you added here was a step forward in your journey.

Fashion is more than fabrics and cuts. It's about storytelling, identity, and creativity. Each exercise you completed brought you closer to refining your unique style and building confidence in your craft.

Remember: growth comes with consistency. Keep sketching, exploring, and above all-have fun with your art.

We'd Love to Hear From You!

If this sketchbook inspired you, please take a moment to share your feedback. Your story can help other aspiring designers discover this book and begin their own creative journey.

Thank you for being part of this adventure!
Keep sketching, keep designing,
and never stop expressing your vision!

Niky Jadesson

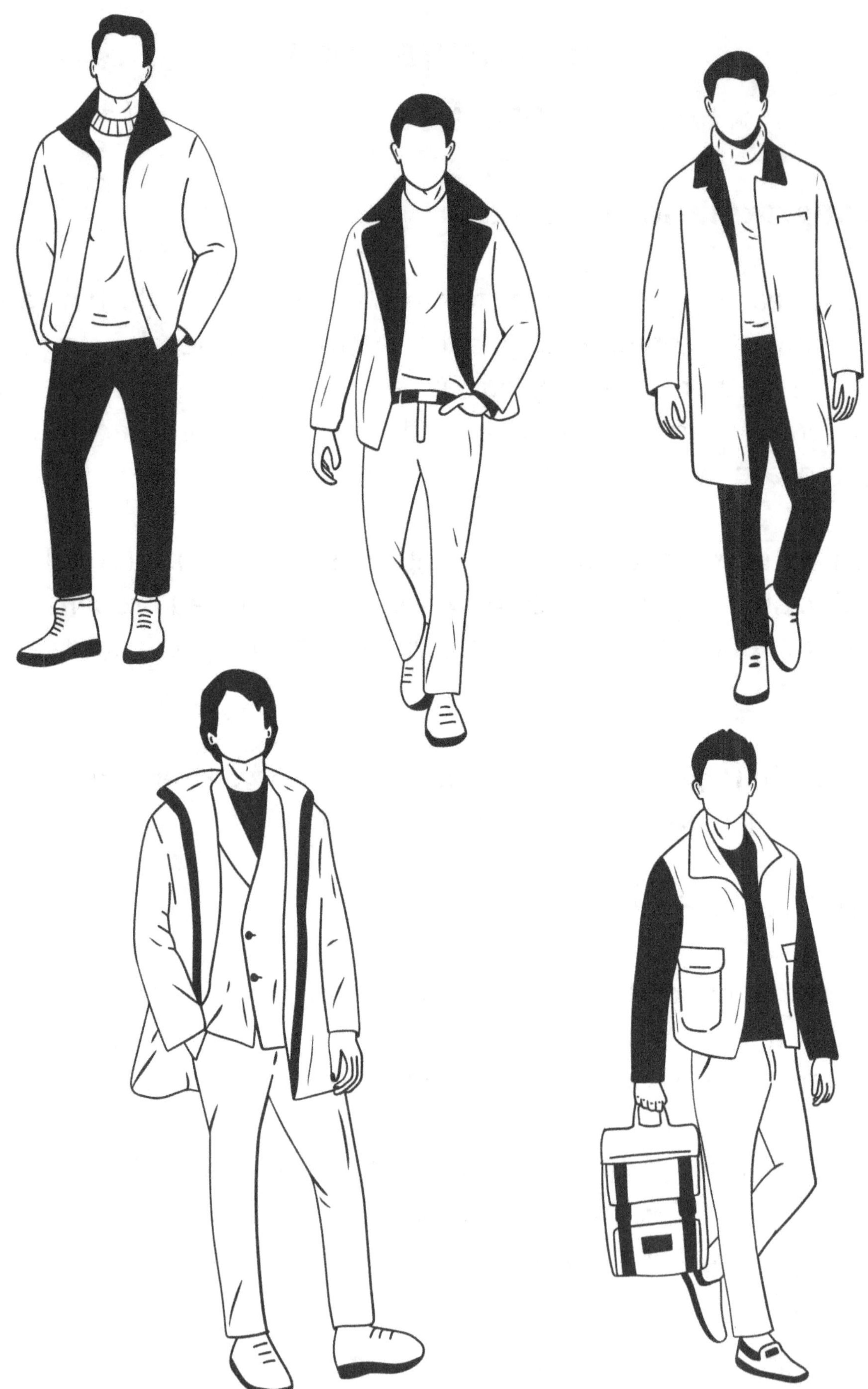

Thank You!

(final message)

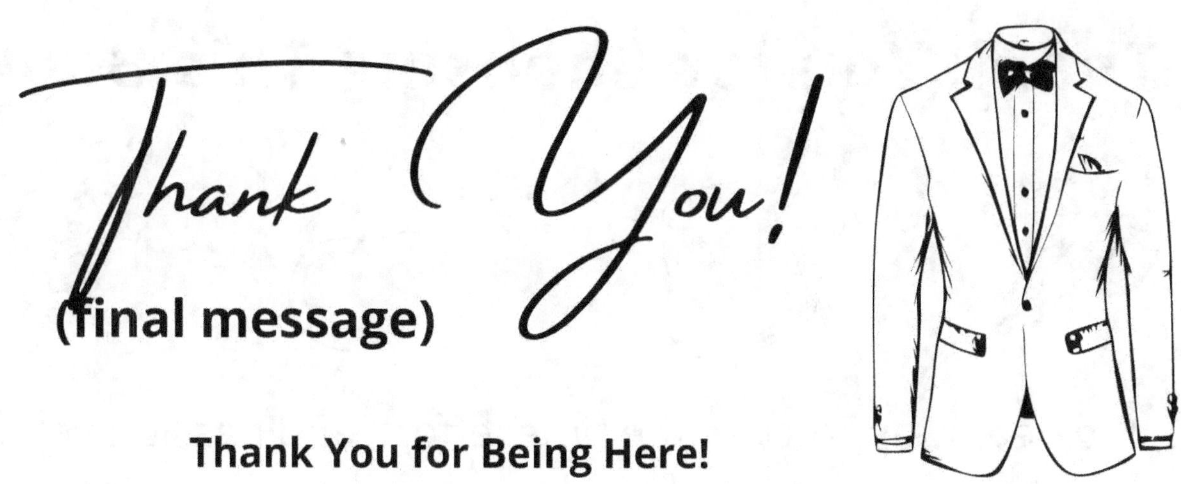

Thank You for Being Here!

We hope you enjoyed this sketchbook and found it inspiring, practical, and fun to use.

Your support means the world to us!

As an independent publishing project, every review, kind word, or suggestion helps us continue creating more tools for aspiring fashion designers like you.

If you'd like to share feedback, suggestions, or simply say hello, we'd love to hear from you:

nikyjadesson@gmail.com

You can also discover more design variations of this sketchbook by searching **Niky Jadesson Books.**

Thank you again for being part of this design work journey-may your artistry continue to shine with every new sketch you bring to life!

Niky Jadesson

Thank You for Choosing This Book!

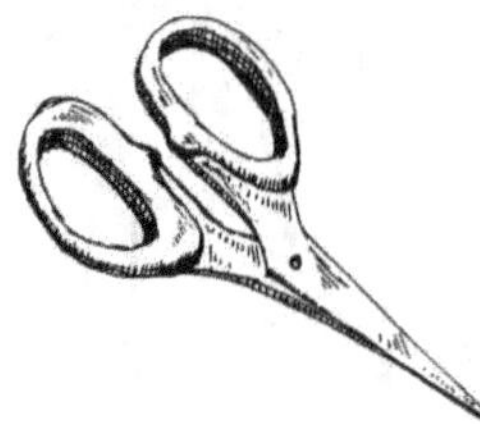 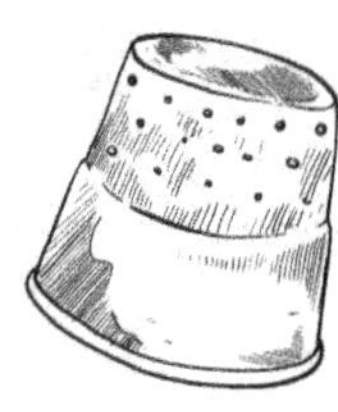 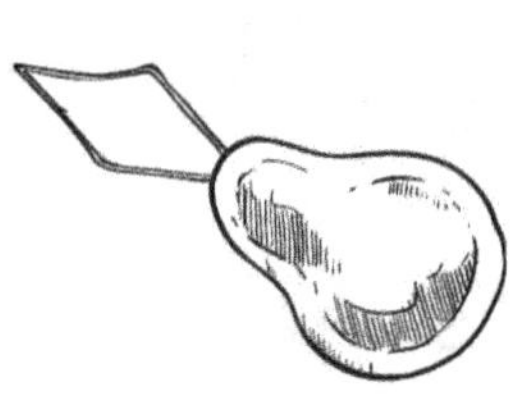 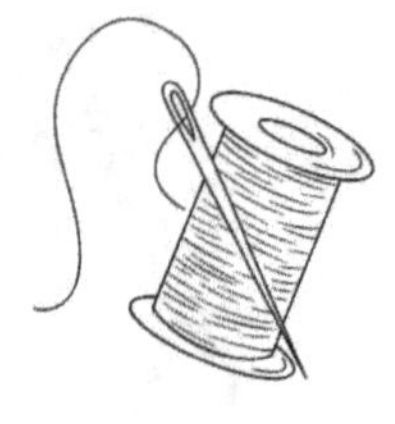

We deeply appreciate the time, effort, and passion you've put into using this sketchbook. Your creativity inspires us to keep making resources that encourage growth, confidence, and self-expression.

If you found this book helpful, your review means so much-it helps other creators discover it and supports our mission to share more.

Want to explore more?
You can find other designs and variations by searching for: **Niky Jadesson Books** online.

Thank you again, and most importantly:

Keep sketching, keep designing,
and keep creating!

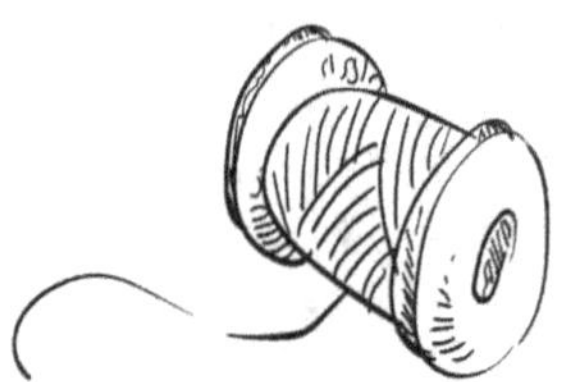

Niky Jadesson

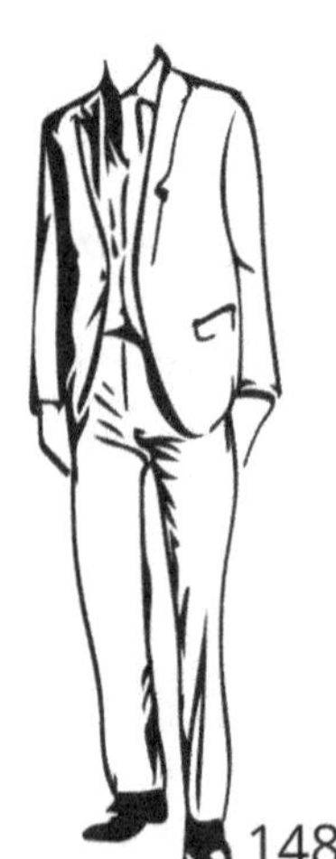

About the Author

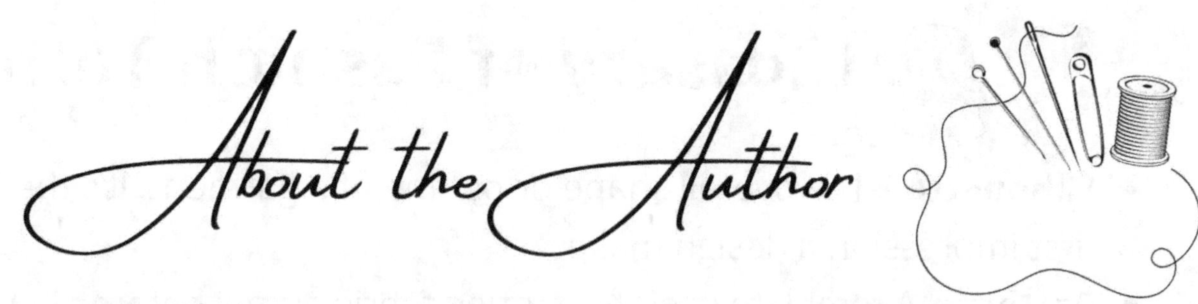

Niky Jadesson is a creative author and designer passionate about blending education with imagination.

With a love for both artistry and self-expression, she creates books that help readers explore their creativity, develop new skills, and enjoy the process along the way.

Her inspiration comes from the joy of learning, the beauty of transformation, and the spark of confidence that comes with practice.

When Niky isn't writing or designing new projects, she enjoys nature walks, sipping tea, and brainstorming fresh ways to make learning and creativity more fun.

Her mission is simple: to inspire and empower people to express themselves, one page at a time.

Her publishing projects include both women's and men's fashion sketchbooks designed to inspire all levels of creators.

Discover more by searching: **Niky Jadesson Books**

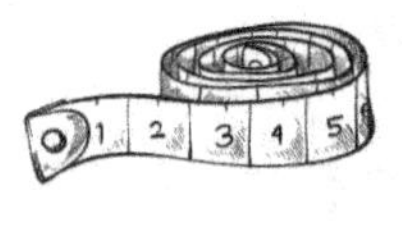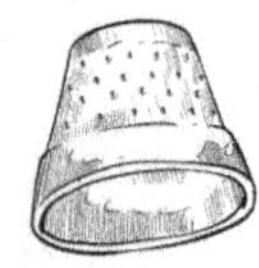 Glossary of Fashion Terms

- **Silhouette** – The overall shape or outline of a garment. It's the first impression a design makes.
- **Pattern** – A template used for cutting fabric pieces before assembling a garment.
- **Drape** – The way fabric falls and moves on a body or mannequin.
- **Seam** – The stitched line where two pieces of fabric are joined.
- **Hemline** – The bottom edge of a garment, usually finished to prevent fraying.
- **Bodice** – The upper section of a garment that covers the torso.
- **Waistline** – The line where the bodice meets the lower garment, defining proportion.
- **Lapels** – The folded flaps on a jacket or coat front.
- **Tailoring** – The art of designing and constructing fitted men's garments.
- **Suiting Fabric** – Textiles like wool, tweed, or linen used in tailored clothing.
- **Lining** – A secondary fabric layer inside a garment for comfort and polish.
- **Textile** – Any woven, knitted, or manufactured fabric used in fashion.
- **Fiber** – The basic material from which fabrics are made (cotton, wool, silk, polyester, etc.).
- **Couture** – Exclusive, custom-made high fashion pieces, often handcrafted.
- **Ready-to-Wear (RTW)** – Clothing produced in standard sizes and sold in stores.
- **Capsule Wardrobe** – A small, versatile collection of essential pieces designed to mix and match.

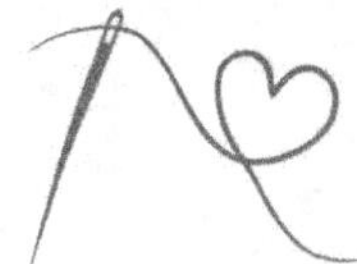 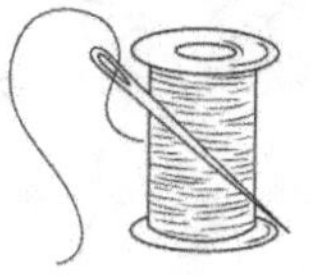

Glossary of Fashion Terms

- **Layering** – Styling by combining multiple garments for depth and flexibility.
- **Color Palette** – The selected set of colors used in a collection or outfit.
- **Trend** – A popular style, detail, or garment shape that dominates fashion at a given time.
- **Moodboard** – A visual collage of images, colors, and textures that inspire a design.
- **Dart** – A stitched fold that shapes fabric to fit the body's curves.
- **Yoke** – A shaped panel (often at the shoulders or hips) that supports the rest of the garment.
- **Bias Cut** – Cutting fabric diagonally across the grain for fluid drape and movement.
- **Trim** – Decorative elements like lace, ribbons, or embroidery.
- **Notions** – Small items like zippers, buttons, snaps, or hooks used in garment construction.
- **Sustainable Fashion** – Clothing designed with environmental and ethical responsibility in mind.
- **Fast Fashion** – Mass-produced, inexpensive clothing inspired by current trends but made quickly.
- **Haute Couture** – The highest standard of fashion craftsmanship, often one-of-a-kind.
- **Collection** – A set of coordinated fashion pieces presented by a designer in one season.

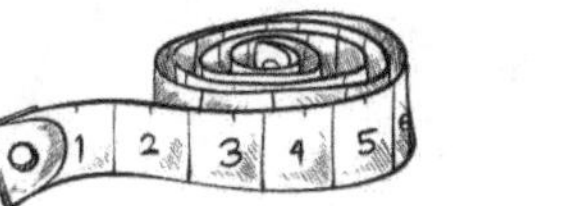